Pro Apache Log4j

Second Edition

SAMUDRA GUPTA

Apress®

Pro Apache Log4j, Second Edition

Copyright © 2005 by Samudra Gupta

ISBN-13: 978-1-59059-499-5
ISBN-10: 1-59059-499-1

Printed and bound in the United States of America (POD)

Trademarked names may appear in this book. Rather than use a trademark symbol with every occurrence of a trademarked name, we use the names only in an editorial fashion and to the benefit of the trademark owner, with no intention of infringement of the trademark.

Java™ and all Java-based marks are trademarks or registered trademarks of Sun Microsystems, Inc. in the US and other countries. Apress, Inc. is not affiliated with Sun Microsystems, Inc., and this book was written without endorsement from Sun Microsystems, Inc.

Lead Editor: Steve Anglin
Technical Reviewer: Jeff Heaton
Editorial Board: Steve Anglin, Dan Appleman, Ewan Buckingham, Gary Cornell, Tony Davis, Jason Gilmore, Jonathan Hassell, Chris Mills, Dominic Shakeshaft, Jim Sumser
Assistant Publisher: Grace Wong
Project Manager: Kylie Johnston
Copy Manager: Nicole LeClerc
Copy Editor: Candace English
Production Manager: Kari Brooks-Copony
Production Editor: Linda Marousek
Compositor: Kinetic Publishing Services, LLC
Proofreader: Linda Marousck
Indexer: Broccoli Information Management
Artist: Kinetic Publishing Services, LLC
Cover Designer: Kurt Krames
Manufacturing Manager: Tom Debolski

Distributed to the book trade in the United States by Springer-Verlag New York, Inc., 233 Spring Street, 6th Floor, New York, NY 10013, and outside the United States by Springer-Verlag GmbH & Co. KG, Tiergartenstr. 17, 69112 Heidelberg, Germany.

In the United States: phone 1-800-SPRINGER, fax 201-348-4505, e-mail orders@springer-ny.com, or visit http://www.springeronline.com. Outside the United States: fax +49 6221 345229, e-mail orders@springer.de, or visit http://www.springer.de.

For information on translations, please contact Apress directly at 2560 Ninth Street, Suite 219, Berkeley, CA 94710. Phone 510-549-5930, fax 510-549-5939, e-mail info@apress.com, or visit http://www.apress.com.

The information in this book is distributed on an "as is" basis, without warranty. Although every precaution has been taken in the preparation of this work, neither the author(s) nor Apress shall have any liability to any person or entity with respect to any loss or damage caused or alleged to be caused directly or indirectly by the information contained in this work.

The source code for this book is available to readers at http://www.apress.com in the Source Code section.

To the lotus feet of Bhagavan Sri Ramakrishna

Contents at a Glance

Contents

About the Author

 **SAMUDRA GUPTA** has more than eight years of experience in Java- and J2EE-related technologies. At present, he is working as a Java/J2EE consultant in the United Kingdom through his own company, SSG Solutions Ltd. His domain expertise is in the public sector tax and national security systems, retail industry, and e-commerce–based applications. He holds a postgraduate degree in information technology and management from All India Management Association, New Delhi, India. Samudra actively contributes articles to Web sites, magazines, and journals such as *JavaWorld* and *Java Developer's Journal*, and is a monthly contributor to JavaBoutique (http://javaboutique.internet.com). When not programming, he loves playing contract bridge and 10-pin bowling.

About the Technical Reviewer

JEFF HEATON (http://www.jeffheaton.com) is an author, college instructor, and consultant. Jeff lives in Chesterfield (St. Louis), Missouri. The author of four books and over two dozen journal and magazine articles, Jeff specializes in Internet, socket-level/spidering, and artificial intelligence programming. He works as a software designer for Reinsurance Group of America (RGA). Jeff is a Sun Certified Java Programmer and a member of the IEEE, and he holds a master's degree in information management from Washington University in St. Louis.

Acknowledgments

Although only one name appears on the cover of this book, the credit for this accomplishment goes to many. I would like to first thank Java editor Steve Anglin for taking up the second edition of this book. Special thanks go to Kylie Johnston, project manager; Candace English, copy editor; and Linda Marousek, production editor, for their splendid job in organizing, copy editing, and production of this book. They have put down a great effort in making this book accurate, timely, and consistent throughout. Without their careful eyes, many mistakes might have made their way into this book.

I am immensely thankful to Jeff Heaton, technical reviewer, who provided many ideas and suggested numerous improvements in this second edition. It feels great to have his name associated with both editions of this book. I must thank Paul Burden and Ashish Patel, two of my esteemed colleagues, for encouraging me to do this second edition by contributing ideas during the course of many discussions.

I take this opportunity to express my deepest gratitude and convey my most humble regards to Professor T.V. Prabhakar, Department of Computer Science and Engineering, Indian Institute of Technology, Kanpur, India, who initiated me into the world of computer science. Without his most valuable and affectionate guidance, it just could not have been the same.

Lastly, my parents and my elder brother (whom I call dadabhai) and my sister-in-law (whom I call boudi) have been a source of constant inspiration and encouragement throughout. I offer them my sincerest regards, and words cannot express my gratitude to them. My wife, Sumita, has encouraged and supported me throughout this period and sacrificed many hours that we could have been together. I thank her for all the support and encouragement.

In the end, I say a big "thank you" to all my friends, too many to name individually; you know who you are.

Introduction

This book is about Apache log4j, the most popular Java-based logging API available in the market. This book deals with the concept of building a flexible and robust application logging framework for Java-based applications and is an in-depth guide to the use of Apache log4j 1.2.9 with an emphasis on the following:

- Understanding the internals of the log4j API and how they work

- Working with the extremely useful, robust logging features available in log4j

- Extending the existing log4j framework for certain specialized application-specific requirements

In recent times, software applications have become more complex and distributed in nature. Time has become the most crucial factor in delivering and supporting any application. Proper logging makes it many times easier to identify and locate problems within applications. Thus, logging is critical to the overall success of any application measured against the maintainability and supportability of the application. The pursuit of a solid logging framework leads to Apache log4j.

Who This Book Is For

This book targets intermediate to advanced Java language application developers. It provides many simple and straightforward examples that demand only minimal familiarity with the Java language. Thus, this book can also be useful to non–Java language programmers, who can still benefit from the ideas presented in this book.

How This Book Is Structured

- Chapter 1, "Introduction to Application Logging": This chapter discusses application logging and describes the advantages and disadvantages related to the various concepts of application logging. The chapter also discusses the criteria of a good logging framework.

- Chapter 2, "Understanding Apache log4j": This chapter provides an in-depth discussion of Apache log4j based on version 1.2.9. It explains the core objects involved in the log4j framework and how they work and interact with each other to finally produce the logging output.

- Chapter 3, "Destination of Logging—The Appender Objects": This chapter discusses the various `Appender` objects available within the log4j API. `Appenders` are responsible for sending the logging information to its destination. The chapter describes in detail how to configure and use each available `Appender` object and provides configuration and usage examples.

- Chapter 4, "Formatting Logging Information in log4j": This chapter discusses the various `Layout` objects available within the log4j API. Layout objects are responsible for formatting the logging information in the desired fashion. It describes in detail how to configure and use each available `Layout` object and provides examples of configuration and usage.

- Chapter 5, "Filtering, Error Handling, and Special Rendering of Log Messages": This chapter discusses the concepts of filtering, error handling, and special rendering of logging information using the tools available within the log4j API. It explains how to use and extend the default log4j components to create application-specific filters, error handlers, and renderers.

- Chapter 6, "Extending log4j to Create Custom Logging Components": This chapter discusses the technology for extending project-specific logging components by extending the existing log4j framework.

- Chapter 7, "A Complete log4j Example": This chapter presents a complete log4j usage example in detail.

- Chapter 8, "Log4j and J2EE": This chapter covers the various issues in using log4j in a J2EE environment and the complexities involved in using log4j within a J2EE container. It also provides guideline solutions with an example WebLogic application server.

- Chapter 9, "Using the Apache Log Tag Library": This chapter discusses the Apache `Log` tag library, which can be used along with JavaSever Pages (JSP) to achieve log4j-based logging activity. It describes the installation and use of the `Log` tag library and shows how to incorporate custom tags within this library.

- Chapter 10, "Best Practices and Looking Forward to 1.3": This chapter discusses the best practices involved in using Apache log4j. It also compares Apache log4j to JDK logging. Finally, this chapter prepares the readers for the forthcoming version 1.3 release of log4j.

- Appendix A, "The log4j Configuration Parameters": This appendix provides a complete list of all the configurable components in log4j and their configuration parameters.

- Appendix B: "The log4j DTD": This appendix provides the complete Document Type Definition (DTD) for the log4j configuration.

Downloading the Code

The source code for this book is available in ZIP file format in the Downloads section of the Apress Web site (`www.apress.com`).

Contacting the Authors

You can reach Samudra Gupta at `guptasamudra@yahoo.co.in`.

CHAPTER 1

■■■

Introduction to Application Logging

Imagine it is late at night and you are still busy debugging your application. Worse—you are debugging another person's code! You have no clue what is wrong with the system. You are not sure where the problem lies. You cannot find any error trace. You do not know what to do, but you do know what is next—the raging managers, the anxious clients—and still it will take time to debug a piece of code without a trace of what is going on.

What is the problem? It is a well-known fact that no software is bug-free. Therefore, we need to assume that application modules may malfunction from time to time, and we need some mechanism to trace what is going wrong. This is precisely the role of application logging. Any commercial application will need logging capability. Debugging an application without any logging trace is time-consuming and costly. Indirectly, a hard-to-debug application loses its market value. Indeed, the impact of well-controlled application logging is multilevel. It improves the quality of the code produced, it increases the maintainability of the application, and all this means more market for the product.

In this chapter, you will see what application logging is and discover its benefits, plus explore a few available Java language–based logging Application Programming Interface(s) (APIs). We will begin with a detailed definition of logging and its value.

What Is Logging?

Logging in any application generally means some way to indicate the state of the system at runtime. However, we all use logging during development to debug and test our modules. The logging activity that should be a part of the application in the deployment phase demands much more thought and care. We almost always want to produce logging that is informative and effective but involves the least possible effort.

Keeping all these points in mind, let's define application logging in the following manner:

Logging is a systematic and controlled way of representing the state of an application in a human-readable fashion.

One important point about logging is that it is *not* synonymous with debugging traces in an application. Logging information can offer more than mere debugging information. However, its usefulness totally depends on how we apply logging within an application. Logging information may be of immense value in analyzing an application's performance. Moreover, we can bundle the application's internal states in logging information and store that information in a structured manner to reuse in the future.

This definition of logging highlights the following important points:

- It is systematic.

- It is controlled.

- It represents an application's state.

In the following sections, we will examine each of these features one by one.

Logging Is Systematic

Logging should be a systematic approach rather than an arbitrary way of producing information. More often than not, we will need to define a strategy for our logging activity. Before we begin, we need to decide what information to log, yet these decisions are not always easy. We should look at this problem from more than one angle. Typically, we need to produce logs for debugging and day-to-day maintenance of an application. We may also need to produce detailed logs for system administrators monitoring the performance of the system. We may need to distribute logging information to various remote places to facilitate remote application management. The issues are endless. Hence, we need a logging strategy before we embark on writing an application.

Logging Is Controlled

There is one and only one way to log the information we require: We have to write some logging code within our applications. The logging code needs to go through the same controls as the main application code. Like every piece of application code, the logging code can be well written or badly written. Keep in mind that logging exists to support and improve the quality of the application being written. Therefore, the logging code should be written in such a way that it has the least possible impact on the overall performance of the system.

Also, we need to control the format of the logging information, and the location where the logging information is stored. The logging information needs to be structured so that is easily readable and can be processed at a future date with minimal effort. One formatting option is to generate logs in XML rather than in simple text. Although the simple text format may be desirable in the development stage, XML is much more reusable and portable when the application is deployed. In regard to storage, we may need to store logging information in a database to maintain a history of the logs produced.

Logging Information Represents the Application State

The logging information the application produces may be quite useless if we don't take sufficient care deciding what to log. To make logging activity most effective, we should aim to represent the internal state of the system wherever required, and also to present a clear idea of the application's stage of control and what the application is doing. If you can visualize your system as a collection of distinct components performing several related and sequential tasks, you may need to log the state of the system before and after each task is performed.

Advantages of Logging

Almost all software development projects run on strict schedules. In this context, incorporating logging code in an application demands extra time and effort. But all software projects are aimed at producing a good end product, and to meet that goal, any application must implement some sort of logging methodology. The benefits of incorporating robust logging in an application make it worthwhile to plan ahead for this capability.

In short, logging within an application can offer the following benefits:

- *Problem diagnosis*: No matter how well written our code is, there may be some problems hidden in it. As soon as the triggering conditions occur, the hidden problems come to the surface. If our applications have well-written code for logging the internal state of the system, we will be able to detect the problems precisely and quickly.

- *Quick debugging*: Once we diagnose the problem, we know exactly how to solve the problem. The logging trace should be aimed at showing the precise location of the problem, which means we will be able to debug the application in less time. Well-planned and well-written logging code greatly reduces the overall cost of debugging the application.

- *Easy maintenance*: Applications with a good logging feature are easy to debug and therefore easy to maintain compared to any application without a similar logging feature. The logging information typically contains more information than the debugging trace.

- *History*: A good logging feature in an application results in logging information being preserved in a structured way at a desired location. The location may be a file, database, or remote machine. All this enables system administrators to retrieve the logging information at a future date by going through the logging history.

- *Cost and time savings*: As explained, well-written logging code offers quick debugging, easy maintenance, and structured storage of an application's runtime information. This makes installation, day-to-day maintenance, and debugging much more cost- and time-effective.

Disadvantages of Logging

In the previous section, we discussed the benefits of logging. In reality, these benefits do not come without a cost. Some disadvantages are inherent in the logging activity, and some may arise from improper use of logging. Whatever the case, the following disadvantages can occur with any logging process:

- Logging adds runtime overhead due to the generation of logging information and the device Input/Output (I/O) related to publishing logging information.

- Logging adds programming overhead due to the extra code required for producing logging information. The logging process increases the size of the code.

- Badly produced logging information can cause confusion.

- Badly written logging code can seriously affect the application's performance.

- Last but not least, logging requires planning ahead, as adding logging code at a late stage of development is difficult.

Despite the disadvantages involved, logging is one of the essential elements of producing quality applications. Carefully planned and well-written logging code will often remove some of the demerits that might otherwise be prominent in poorly programmed logging code.

How Logging Works

In the previous sections I discussed the process, advantages, and disadvantages associated with logging. We all want to write an application with a well-designed logging feature. But the question is how to achieve an effective logging mechanism.

You are probably acquainted with the most familiar Java syntax, `System.out.println()`, and you might know the famous `printf()` command in the C language. These produce a piece of information that is printed to a console, and they represent the most primitive type of logging that can be embedded within an application. Such items will produce what we want in a nice and simple fashion. But they defeat the purpose of controlled logging in that there is no way we can turn off any of these statements.

You might be wondering why you need to turn off logging statements when you put so much effort into including them. A complex application may have complicated logging activities. One goal of logging may be to produce enough information about the internal state and functioning of the system. Another goal may be to produce enough detail that in case of malfunction the problem can be detected and debugged quickly. On a good day, when an application is running without any problems, any debugging-related logging information appearing in the logging trace may prevent the logging information from being clean and easily understandable. So we need some mechanism to turn off the debug-related logging trace. On a not-so-good day, we may wish to turn on the debug-related logging to see exactly what is going wrong.

The normal `System.out.println()` logging methodology is not capable of offering such flexibility, because it does not provide a way to modify the behavior of the static logging code. Even if we accept that we always want to see what we produce, the other problem is that it is very difficult to segregate logging messages into different priority levels. Surely, messages related to a database operation problem are more crucial than messages showing entry and exist to and from a method.

In essence, a robust logging framework means that the messages should be categorized in terms of their severity. Also, we should be able to switch over to any severity level to see messages with only that level of severity. But this sort of flexibility should not mean changes to the source code. We need to achieve this flexibility via configuration parameters. Thus, a good logging system needs to be highly configurable.

It is also very important that we be able to redirect logging information to a chosen destination, such as a database, file, etc., so that we can reuse that information. Console-based logging activity is limited; it is volatile, as the logging information is not stored anywhere for future reference. A robust logging framework should offer flexibility in terms of the logging destination and message formatting.

While it is true that a good logging API will provide a flexible, robust, and feature-rich logging environment, it also demands appropriate and efficient use of all these logging features. In this book, we will examine basic logging techniques with Apache log4j. Chapter 10 will focus on the best practices involved in using Apache log4j.

From the architectural point of view, software application modules and logging components reside in two separate layers. The application makes a call to the logging components in the logging layer and delegates the logging responsibility to those components. The logging components receive the logging request and publish the logging information at preferred destinations. Figure 1-1 represents the collaboration of a software module and its logging components.

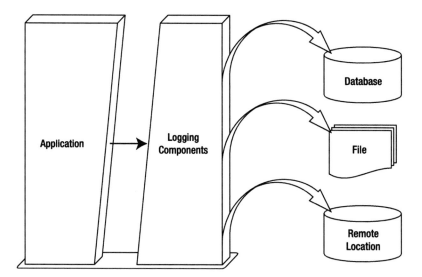

Figure 1-1. *The application logging process*

As shown in the figure, the logging components have the freedom to publish logging information to any destination of choice, such as a file, database, or remote location. The logging components can, in turn, use any other available technologies to achieve localized and distributed logging.

Evaluating a Logging Package

In a large-scale development process, it is crucial that we implement a proper logging mechanism. Whether we develop the logging component in-house or use a third-party logging component, we must evaluate the logging components against certain criteria. In a nutshell, the following criteria are features of a good logging package:

- *Configuration*: Logging components may support programmatic and file-based configuration. The latter is better, as it allows us to avoid changing our source code to switch to a different type of logging behavior. Also, the logging package should support dynamic configuration as opposed to static configuration. Dynamic configuration enables us to change logging behavior without taking down an application.

- *Flexibility*: A logging package should provide flexibility in terms of what to log and where to log. Also, we should be able to prioritize logging information based on its level of importance. We require a logging package that supports multiple loggers and multiple levels of messages, and is capable of publishing logging messages to various destinations.

- *Output*: The way that a logging package can output logging information to a preferred destination is important for the success of the package. We must carefully consider how flexible the logging package is in terms of output formats and destinations.

- *Ease of use*: However good the design of a logging package may be, if it is not easy to use, chances are that anyone working on or using the application will not use it. So we need to evaluate any logging package in terms of its ease of use.

Popular Java-Based Logging APIs

Experience has taught people the importance of application logging, and how to write well-designed logging code. Once logging concepts were proven successful, they were put into use as generic logging APIs. A few Java-based logging APIs are available in the market. Some of them are proprietary, and some are open source. Out of all the available APIs, the following are most popular in the Java community.

JDK Logging API

JDK has its own logging API in its `java.util.logging` package. This API originated from the JSR 47. The JDK logging API is, in essence, a scaled-down version of Apache log4j (discussed in the next section). The logging concepts captured in this API involve logging levels and different logging destinations and formats. The JDK logging API is well suited for simple applications with simple logging requirements. Despite a few limitations, this API provides all the basic features that you need to produce effective logging information.

Apache log4j

Apache log4j is an open-source logging API. This API, which evolved from the E.U. SEMPER (Secure Electronic Marketplace for Europe) project, is a popular logging package in Java. It allows great control over the granularity of logging statements. A main benefit of this API is that it is highly configurable through external configuration files at runtime. It views the logging process in terms of levels of priorities and offers mechanisms to direct logging information to a great variety of destinations, such as a database, file, console, Windows NT event log, UNIX Syslog, Java Message Service (JMS), and so on. It also allows application developers to choose from various formatting styles, such as XML, HTML, etc.

Overall, log4j is a feature-rich, well-designed extendible logging framework, and provides more capabilities than the JDK logging API. For example, the configuration of log4j is much more flexible than that of the JDK logging API. The JDK logging API can be configured only through a properties-style configuration file, but log4j supports both properties- and XML-style configuration.

In this book, Chapters 2 through 9 are devoted exclusively to log4j. Chapter 10 will present a comparison between the log4j and JDK logging API.

Commons Logging API

The Commons logging API is another logging effort from Apache. The goal of this API is to provide a seamless transition from one logging API to another. Depending upon the presence of a logging framework in the classpath, the Commons logging API will try to use the available API to carry out application logging. The Commons logging API runs its own discovery process to find out which logging API is available in the classpath. It tends to provide the lowest common denominator of any two logging APIs. For example, between log4j and the JDK logging API, it will provide a seamless transition for the features common in both—so we would miss any extra features used in log4j.

In terms of operation, the Commons logging API creates a wrapper for all the objects in the logging API. Automatic discovery and wrapper generation are heavyweight processes and tend to slow down the overall performance. This is a more complex logging framework compared to the JDK logging API or Apache log4j, as this API tries to combine the efforts of more than one logging API. Commons offers the flexibility to switch between different logging APIs without changing the source code. But before using it, determine whether you need such flexibility at the cost of added complexity and performance degradation due to the heavyweight nature of the Commons logging API.

The Commons logging API represents a great effort to offer a common logging interface; it enables an application to switch to different logging APIs without changes to the application code. Once you understand and appreciate the methodologies that the JDK and Apache log4j logging APIs adopt, you'll be able to understand the philosophy behind the Commons logging API. Therefore, we will not discuss the Commons logging API further in this book.

The Road Ahead

This book is dedicated solely to the discussion of Apache log4j based on version 1.2.9, the latest at the time this book was written. This book will also note the changes and additions anticipated in version 1.3, which is lurking just around the corner. The foundation and the architecture of log4j shall remain the same; the changes mainly incorporate more features into this wonderful API. When you have mastered the basics of Apache log4j, you'll have no problem transitioning to the new version.

## CHAPTER 2

Understanding Apache log4j

The Apache log4j implementation is a highly scalable, robust, and versatile logging framework. This API simplifies the writing of logging code within an application, yet allows the flexibility of controlling logging activity from an external configuration file. It also allows us to publish logging information to desired granularity depending on the detail of the logging information suitable to each application.

We can tailor the granularity of logging activity suitable for the development phase or the deployment phase of an application without having to change the source code. It is possible to switch over to a different logging behavior by only changing a few configuration parameters.

Apache log4j is also capable of publishing logging information to various destinations such as files, consoles, and NT event logs. Moreover, logging information can even be distributed over Java Message Service (JMS) or Java Database Connectivity (JDBC), or can be output to a TCP/IP socket. This API lets us take logging information and publish or print it in different formats and layouts that are human-readable and reusable by any error-handling and analyzer program. The scalability aspect of log4j allows developers to enhance the capability of logging by creating new logging destinations and unique formats and layouts.

Although using the log4j framework is easy, it demands certain methods and practices be adopted for the best possible results. In this chapter, we will discuss the overall architecture of the log4j framework and different objects within the API, and examine in detail the application and usage of the core logging objects.

Installing log4j

Apache log4j is an open-source project from Apache. You must meet the following criteria to successfully install and use log4j:

- Get the latest version of the log4j binary distribution from http://jakarta.apache.org/log4j. The examples and concepts in this book are based on the log4j version 1.2.9 release. You may obtain any later version of log4j, if available, and still be able to follow the examples in this book.

- Apache log4j is JDK 1.1.x compatible. Make sure you have the appropriate JDK version downloaded to your machine. Any version of JDK can be downloaded from http://java.sun.com.

- You need a JAXP-compatible XML parser to use log4j. Make sure you have Xerces.jar installed on your machine.

Caution The latest version of Xerces requires you to download JDK 1.2.x.

- The e-mail–based logging feature in log4j requires the Java Mail API (`mail.jar`) to be installed on your machine. Apache log4j is tested against version 1.2 of the Java Mail API.

- The Java Mail API will also require that the JavaBeans Activation Framework (`activation.jar`) be installed on your machine.

- The JMS-compatible features of log4j will require that both JMS and JNDI (Java Naming and Directory Interface) be installed on your machine.

Once you have acquired and installed all the required `.jar` files, you must make sure that all these resources are available within the classpath of the Java runtime.

Overview of the log4j Architecture

The architecture of the log4j API is layered. Each layer consists of different objects performing different tasks. The top layer captures the logging information, the middle layer is involved in analyzing and authorizing the logging information, and the bottom layer is responsible for formatting and publishing the logging information to a destination. In essence, log4j consists of three types of primary objects:

- Logger: The `Logger` object (known as the `Category` object in releases prior to log4j 1.2) is responsible for capturing logging information. `Logger` objects are stored in a namespace hierarchy. I'll discuss this topic further in the "Logger Object" section of this chapter.

- Appender: The `Appender` object is responsible for publishing logging information to various preferred destinations. Each `Appender` object will have at least one target destination attached to it. For example, a `ConsoleAppender` object is capable of printing logging information to a console.

- Layout: The `Layout` object is used to format logging information in different styles. `Appender` objects utilize `Layout` objects before publishing logging information. `Layout` objects play an important role in publishing logging information in a way that is human-readable and reusable.

The preceding core objects are central to the architecture of log4j. Apart from them, there are several auxiliary objects that can plug and play to any layer of the API. These objects help manage the different `Logger` objects active within an application and fine-tune the logging process.

Next, let's go over the principal auxiliary components in the log4j framework that play a vital role in the logging framework:

- Level: The `Level` object, previously referred to as the `Priority` object, defines the granularity and priority of any logging information. Each piece of logging information is accompanied by its appropriate `Level` object, which tells the `Logger` object about the priority of the information. There are seven levels of logging defined within the API: OFF, DEBUG, INFO, ERROR, WARN, FATAL, and ALL. Each level has a unique integer value. The `Level` values can be arranged in an ascending manner:

    ALL<DEBUG<INFO<WARN<ERROR<FATAL<OFF

where ALL means most of the logging information will be published and OFF means none of the logging information will be published. For more on this topic, see the "Level Object" section.

- Filter: The Filter object is used to analyze logging information and make further decisions on whether that information should be logged or not. In the log4j context, Appender objects can have several Filter objects associated with them. If logging information is passed to a particular Appender object, all the Filter objects associated with that Appender need to approve the logging information before it can be published to the preferred destination attached to the Appender. Filter objects are very helpful in filtering out unwanted logging information based on any application-specific criteria.

- ObjectRenderer: The ObjectRenderer object is specialized in providing a String representation of different objects passed to the logging framework. More precisely, when the application passes a custom Object to the logging framework, the logging framework will use the corresponding ObjectRenderer to obtain a String representation of the passed Object. This is used by Layout objects to prepare the final logging information.

- LogManager: The LogManager object manages the logging framework. It is responsible for reading the initial configuration parameters from a system-wide configuration file or a configuration class. The LogManager stores in a namespace hierarchy each Logger instance created with a namespace within an application. When we try to obtain the reference named logger, the LogManager class returns the already created instance of it, or creates a new instance of the named logger, stores it in a repository for future reference, and returns the new instance to the caller application. We shall discuss more on this topic in the "LogManager Object" section of this chapter.

Now that you have seen the log4j core components, it is time to briefly discuss how they interact with each other.

- The central part of the log4j framework is the Logger object.

- An application instantiates a named Logger instance and passes various logging information to it.

- A Logger object has a designated Level object associated with it. The Logger object provides several logging methods that are capable of logging information into categorized levels.

- A Logger logs only the messages with Level objects equal to or greater than its assigned Level object, or else it rejects the logging request.

- Once the Level condition has been met, the Logger object passes the logging information to all its associated Appender objects and to all the Appender objects associated with its parent Logger, recursively up the logging hierarchy.

- Similar to Logger objects, Appender objects can also have threshold Levels attached to them. The logging information is validated against the threshold Level attached to the Appender. If the log message has a Level equal to or greater than the threshold Level, the logging message is passed to the next stage.

- The Appender objects then look for any Filter object associated with them. If there are any, the logging information is passed through all the Filter objects in a chain.

- Once all the Filter objects approve a message, the Appender utilizes any Layout object associated with it to format the message, and finally it publishes the logging information to the preferred destination.

Figure 2-1 depicts the overall flow of the log4j logging architecture in a UML sequence diagram.

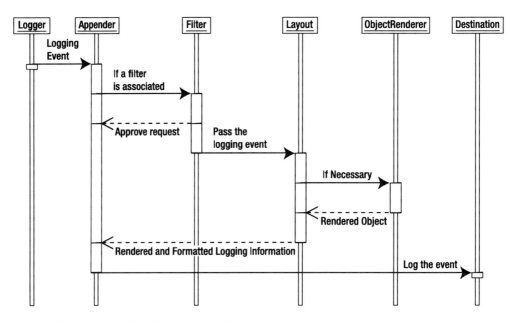

Figure 2-1. *Overview of the log4j framework*

So far, we have seen the interaction between different objects in the log4j framework. All these different objects and their properties are supplied to the log4j framework in a configuration file. At the startup of any application, this configuration file is supplied to the log4j framework either programmatically or as a command line parameter. In the next section, we will learn how to configure log4j.

Configuring log4j

Before we can use log4j in an application, we need to configure log4j in an application-specific manner. You can decide to configure log4j programmatically or through a configuration file depending on your requirement. However, having a configuration file offers much more flexibility in terms of changing and managing the logging functionalities without having to change any source code. In fact, configuring log4j through a configuration file is so popular that I have never seen anyone willing to even bother about programmatic configuration. Therefore, we will discuss the configuration of log4j only through configuration files.

Configuring log4j typically involves assigning Level objects, defining Appender objects, and specifying Layout objects. The configuration information is conventionally defined within a properties file in a key-value pattern. It is also possible to define the log4j configuration in an XML format, which we will discuss later in this section.

Naming and Placing the Configuration File

By default, the LogManager class will look for a file named log4j.properties or log4j.xml in the classpath used for loading the log4j classes.

■**Note** Up to version 1.2.6, log4j would look for only the `log4j.properties` file in the classpath. Since version 1.2.7, log4j looks for both `log4j.properties` and `log4j.xml` in the classpath.

If you decide to name your configuration file differently, you are free to do that. However, you have to let the log4j framework know by supplying a command line argument as follows:

`-Dlog4j.configuration="file_name".`

We'll return to this topic later in this chapter when discussing initialization of log4j.

What We Can Configure

In general, we are looking to configure each `Logger` and each `Appender` associated with it. The `Appender` object can have other objects such as `Layout` associated with it. Table 2-1 explains most of the configurable properties associated with the log4j objects.

Table 2-1. *An Overview of the Configurable Parameters in log4j*

Logger	Appender	Layout	Filter	ErrorHandler
`Appender-ref:` Reference for the appenders to use	`Layout:` The layout pattern to publish the logging messages	`Class:` The class that implements this layout	`Class:` Class implementing a particular filter	`Logger-ref:` The Logger that this ErrorHandler should be used against
`Level:` Level of the logging	`Error-handler:` Any special error handler	`Param:` Any parameter specific to a particular layout to format the logging messages	`Param:` Any parameter specific to a filter	`Appender-ref:` The Appender that this ErrorHandler should be used against
`Name:` Name of the Logger	`Filter:` Any filter for specialized filtering of the log messages			`Class:` Implementing class of the ErrorHandler
`Additivity:` True/false; indicates whether to delegate logging calls to the parent loggers	`Appender-ref:` Any other nested appender to which the log messages should be forwarded			
	`Name:` Name of the appender			
	`Class:` A particular implementation class of the appender			

Table 2-1 outlines different configuration elements for log4j. This table does not present all the available configuration parameters for each object in log4j. I will expand on the set of configuration parameters when I discuss individual log4j components. Additionally, a complete list of configurable parameters appears in Appendix A.

Let's look at a sample configuration file. Listing 2-1 shows a simple log4j configuration. It defines the level and appender for the root logger. You can name this file log4j.properties and place it in the application's classpath. The log4j framework will pick up any log4j. properties file in the classpath.

Listing 2-1. *A Simple log4j Configuration File*

```
#set the level of the root logger to DEBUG and set its appender
#as an appender named testAppender
log4j.rootLogger = DEBUG, testAppender
#define a named logger
log4j.logger.dataAccessLogger = com.apress.logging.logger

#set the appender named testAppender to be a console appender
log4j.appender.testAppender=org.apache.log4j.ConsoleAppender

#set the layout for the appender testAppender
log4j.appender.testAppender.layout=org.apache.log4j.PatternLayout
log4j.appender.testAppender.layout.conversionPattern=%m%n
```

The preceding configuration defines the level of the root logger as DEBUG and specifies the appender to use as testAppender. Next, we define the appender testAppender as referencing the org.apache.log4j.ConsoleAppender object and specify the layout of the appender as org.apache.log4j.PatternLayout. A PatternLayout also requires that a conversion pattern or a format be supplied. We supply the conversion pattern %m%n in this case, which means the logging message will be printed followed by a newline character.

▓**Note** Within the conversion pattern, %m represents the message string and %n represents a newline character. You will learn more about these conversion patterns in Chapter 4.

A more complex configuration can attach multiple appenders to a particular logger. Each appender, in turn, can have a different layout, and that layout can have a conversion pattern associated with it. Listing 2-2 is an example of a more complex configuration file.

Listing 2-2. *Complex log4j Configuration File*

```
# define the root logger with two appenders writing to console and file
log4j.rootLogger = DEBUG, CONSOLE, FILE

#define your own logger named com.foo
#and assign level and appender to your own logger

log4j.logger.com.foo=DEBUG,FILE

#define the appender named FILE
log4j.appender.FILE=org.apache.log4j.FileAppender
log4j.appender.FILE.File=${user.home}/log.out
```

```
#define the appender named CONSOLE
log4j.appender.CONSOLE=org.apache.log4j.ConsoleAppender
log4j.appender.CONSOLE.conversionPattern=%m%n
```

This configuration file defines the root logger as having level DEBUG and attaches two appenders named CONSOLE and FILE to it. We define one of our own custom loggers with the name com.foo and the level DEBUG and attach an appender named FILE to the custom logger. The appender FILE is defined as org.apache.log4j.FileAppender. The FILE appender writes to a file named log.out located in the user.home system path.

It is important to note that log4j supports UNIX-style variable substitution such as ${variableName}. The variable name defined is considered as the key and searched first in the system properties. If the log4j framework does not find the name, it then looks for the value for the variable in the properties file being parsed. The CONSOLE appender is then assigned to the org.apache.log4j.ConsoleAppender and the conversion pattern defined is %m%n, which means the printed logging message will be followed by a newline character.

XML-Style Configuration

With log4j, it is possible to define configuration parameters in an XML file and pass that file to the application at startup to configure different logging components. The XML configuration follows a document type definition (DTD) named log4j.dtd, which is detailed in Appendix B. The configuration parameters and values are described in tag formats. For example, the configuration information in Listing 2-1 can be defined in XML format as follows:

```xml
<?xml version="1.0" encoding="UTF-8" ?>
<!DOCTYPE log4j:configuration SYSTEM "log4j.dtd">
<log4j:configuration>
<appender name="dataAccessLogger" class="org.apache.log4j.ConsoleAppender">
    <layout class="org.apache.log4j.PatternLayout">
        <param name="conversionPattern" value="%m%n"/>
    </layout>
  </appender>

<logger name="com.apress.logging.log4j" additivity="false">
   <level value="debug"/>
   <appender-ref ref="dataAccessLogger"/>
</logger>
  <root>
    <priority value ="debug" />
    <appender-ref ref="dataAccessLogger"/>
  </root>

</log4j:configuration>
```

Both the XML-style configuration and properties-style configuration are quite effective in configuring log4j. Both are flexible and good configuration styles. However, a few components in log4j, such as Filter, AsyncAppender, etc., can be configured only through XML-style configuration. It seems that log4j is evolving from properties-style configuration toward XML-style configuration, and gradually it will embrace XML-style configuration as the standard. For the time being, you need to master both configuration styles.

Notable Points About Configuration

Irrespective of how you configure log4j, keep in mind the following points:

- The configuration is case-sensitive.

- A few of the appenders, such as AsyncAppender, can be configured only through an XML file.

- Some advanced controls, such as Filter and ObjectRenderer, can be configured only via an XML file.

Log4j Initialization

In general, log4j makes no assumption about the environment it is running in. Therefore, it is the application developer's responsibility to configure log4j. Configuring log4j essentially means specifying loggers, appenders, layouts, etc. The LogManager class performs the initialization operation at startup only once through a class-level static initializer block. The default initialization operation consists of the following steps:

1. The LogManager class looks for the system property log4j.configuration.

2. If the log4j.configuration property is not defined, then it tries to look for a resource named log4j.properties/log4j.xml in the application classpath.

3. It then attempts to convert the defined configuration resource string to a URL object. If the resource string cannot be converted into a valid java.net.URL object, then it throws a java.net.MalformedURLException.

4. If no resource can be found, the initialization is aborted.

5. If the resource is found and if it is a normal Java properties-style file containing configuration information in a key-value format, then the org.apache.log4j.PropertyConfigurator class is used to parse the configuration file. If the configuration file is an XML file, the org.apache.log4j.xml.DOMConfigurator class is used to parse the XML file and initialize the logging objects.

It is possible to avoid the default initialization classes such as LogManager and write your own configuration class. The custom configuration class can be specified as a log4j.configurationClass to the Java runtime at application startup. Any custom configuration class should implement the org.apache.log4j.spi.Configurator interface by default.

Initialization Through VM Parameters

Log4j accepts three separate virtual machine (VM) parameters in the initialization process. They are as follows:

- log4j.configuration: Specifies the log4j configuration file.

- log4j.configurationClass: Specifies any customized initialization class to use instead of the default configuration class LogManager in log4j.

- log4j:defaultInitOverride: Overrides the default initialization process. If set to true, the default log4j initialization process is no longer valid. If set to false, the log4j default initialization process continues following the values specified for the VM parameters already outlined.

- log4j.debug: Variable that indicates whether the log4j internal logging should be enabled. It is sometimes useful to see how log4j is initializing itself.

For example, we can pass the configuration file and configuration class respectively to the Java runtime with the following commands:

```
java -Dlog4j.configuration=config file yourApp
java -Dlog4j.configurationClass=config class yourApp
```

Creating a Log4j Configuration File

We will now see how to write a small program that will print very basic logging information with the help of a Logger object. We will create our own configuration properties file as defined in Listing 2-3, give it the name log4j.properties, and pass it to the Java runtime as a system property.

Note I am favoring properties-style configuration because it is easy to follow. When you start using advanced log4j components, you will use XML-style configuration files as some of the advanced log4j components can be configured only via XML-style configuration files.

Listing 2-3. *log4j.properties*

```
#set the level of the root logger to DEBUG (the lowest level) and
#set its appender
#as an appender named testAppender
log4j.rootLogger = DEBUG, testAppender

#set your own logger
log4j.logger.com.apress.logging.log4j=DEBUG,testAppender

#set the appender named testAppender to be a console appender
log4j.appender.testAppender=org.apache.log4j.ConsoleAppender

#set the layout for the appender testAppender
log4j.appender.testAppender.layout=org.apache.log4j.PatternLayout
log4j.appender.testAppender.layout.conversionPattern=%p-%m%n
```

In this configuration file, we have defined our own logger, com.apress.logging.log4j, and assigned it the level DEBUG and the appender testAppender. The appender testAppender is again defined to be an org.apache.log4j.ConsoleAppender with a conversion pattern of %m%n, which means the logging message will be followed by a newline character and printed to its default output stream, System.out. The %p sign will print the level of the logging message as a part of the output. Please refer to Chapter 4 for a detailed discussion on the different formatting options available.

The program in Listing 2-4, SimpleLogging.java, is intended to print a simple debugging message. The main point to take away is that the Logger will be configured through the log4j.properties file defined in Listing 2-3.

Listing 2-4. *SimpleLogging.java*

```java
package com.apress.logging.log4j;

import org.apache.log4j.*;

public class SimpleLogging {
    /** Creates a new instance of SimpleLogging */
    public SimpleLogging() {
    }

    /**
     * @param args the command line arguments
     */
    public static void main(String[] args) {
        Logger logger =
Logger.getLogger(SimpleLogging.class.getPackage().getName());
        logger.info("Hello this is an info message");
    }
}
```

One important item to note in this simple program is how we obtain the Logger object reference. We create a logger with a namespace the same as the package name of the class, which in this case is com.apress.logging.log4j. I will provide detail on the strategy for creating a logger namespace in the "Logger Object" section of this chapter. For the time being, it is enough to notice that in the configuration file we have created a logger with the same name as the package name (com.apress.logging.log4j) of the SimpleLogging class. Once we get hold of the logger within the main() method, we then call the info() method on the Logger object to print the message.

Running the Program

We are now ready to run this program. It is important to make sure the classpath system variable contains all the classes as well as the log4j.properties file. We can then run the program with the following command by passing the name of the configuration file to load as a system parameter:

```
java -Dlog4j.configuration=log4j.properties com.apress.logging.log4j.SimpleLogging
```

The appender attached to the obtained logger is org.apache.log4j.ConsoleAppender. Hence, the program in Listing 2-4 will print the following message to the console:

```
INFO-Hello this is an info message
INFO-Hello this is an info message
```

Why the Message Printed Twice

You may be wondering why the same information is printed twice. The simple answer is that the message is printed twice because it is propagated to both the named logger and the root logger for handling. Both loggers have printed the message through their respective appenders. We can switch off this feature by setting the additivity flag of the named logger to false.

```
log4j.additivity.com.apress.logging.log4j=false
```

Consult the "Logger Object" section of this chapter for more detail on this feature.

Configuring log4j Programmatically

Apache log4j allows us to configure the logging framework programmatically without specifying any system property. As mentioned earlier, the properties-style configuration files are parsed with the org.apache.log4j.PropertyConfigurator object; we can use the same object within an application to read and parse the configuration file. For example, in the program in Listing 2-4, we could have used the following to configure the logging framework:

```
public  static void main(String args[])
  {
      PropertyConfigurator.configure(args[0]);
  }
```

where args[0] is the name of the configuration file supplied as a command line parameter. This will also configure the framework correctly by reading any configuration file specified. The only important thing to note about this method is that ideally the configuration should be loaded at the entry point of the application, such as in the main() method. Otherwise, the application might be loading the configuration information several times and slow down performance. For example, if you want to initialize log4j within a servlet, the best way to do that is inside the init() method of the servlet, which will be called only once. Likewise, the initialization will take place only once.

In a more simplistic situation, the Logger object can assume a very basic configuration through the org.apache.log4j.BasicConfigurator class.

```
BasicConfigurator.configure()
```

This instruction configures the root logger to a level of DEBUG and assigns org.apache.log4j. ConsoleAppender as the default appender with the conversion pattern %-4r[%t]%-5p%c%x - %m%n. By default, log4j is configured to propagate the logging request up through the logger hierarchy.

■**Note** If we use the default setting in an application, and we obtain our own named logger but do not use any external configuration file to configure it, then it will automatically inherit and use the properties of the root logger set by the BasicConfigurator.

Dynamic Loading of Configuration

If you are configuring the logging framework with an external configuration file, you may have to restart the application every time you change the properties file. To avoid this, both the PropertyConfigurator and the DOMConfigurator classes can implement dynamic loading of the configuration file. The following methods demonstrate this in both configuration classes:

```
public void configureAndWatch(String filename, long delay);
public void configureAndWatch(String filename);
```

These methods use another helper class, `org.apache.log4j.helpers.FileWatchDog`, that determines if the configuration file exists. If the file exists, it then creates a separate thread and searches for any modification in the file after a specified interval or after a default interval of 60 seconds. If the configuration file is modified, then the `Configurator` class re-reads the configuration to configure the logging framework.

This property becomes very useful in the context of server-based applications, where taking down any Web site may be undesirable, yet you need to change the application's logging configuration. The next section provides an example.

▓**Caution** It is not safe to use the `configureAndWatch()` method in the J2EE environment. For more discussion, see Chapter 8.

In the next section, we will learn more about configuring and using log4j in Web applications.

▓**Note** From this point on, we will be using the `log4j.properties` configuration file listed in Listing 2-3 for all examples in this chapter. This is because we will be using the same package structure for all the examples and therefore the same named logger. Any extra configuration information mentioned in relevant sections, such as our discussion on attaching different appenders, will have to be included in the `log4j.properties` unless I state otherwise.

Configuring log4j in Web Applications

The use of log4j is not restricted to standalone applications; it can be widely applied to any type of application deployment environment. In this section, you will see how log4j can be used in Web applications. You'll learn how to initialize log4j in a Web application container and how to use log4j to log messages.

Setting Up Tomcat

In this section, we will demonstrate the use of the Tomcat 3.2.1 Web server configuration under the Windows operating system. You can easily figure out the corresponding files in the UNIX environment to configure Tomcat. You can download Tomcat from `http://jakarta.apache.org/tomcat`. For a detailed discussion on Tomcat, purchase *Pro Jakarta Tomcat 5* by Matthew Moodie (Apress, 2004).

▓**Note** Tomcat is an open-source servlet engine from Apache, rather than a full-scale Web server, and it can be integrated with the Apache Web server. Although we are using Tomcat for the examples in this book, you can experiment with other Web servers that support Java servlets.

First build the example servlet along with the HTML file into a `.war` file and deploy the servlet into a folder named `logdemo` under your default Tomcat directory. After deploying the servlet successfully, you should be able to see your HTML file by entering your Web server URL (`http://localhost:8080/logdemo/logging.html`) in the browser window.

▓**Note** To build a `.war` file, we need to use Ant with a custom build script. A `.war` file, or Web application archive, is a variant of the `.jar` file that Tomcat uses for Web application deployment. Consult the Ant documentation for details on building applications with the tool. Once we have created the `.war` file, we need to drop it in the `/webapps` folder of the Tomcat installation. Once we restart Tomcat, it will automatically extract the files from within the `.war` file.

The following sections describe the two basic ways to configure log4j to work with Tomcat.

Configuring Through a System Parameter

The log4j configuration within the Tomcat environment is not a difficult one. By following the steps described here, we can set up Tomcat to use log4j:

1. Pass the `log4j.properties` file as a system variable to the Tomcat's execution environment.

2. Go to the `tomcat.bat` file in `%TOMCAT_HOME%\bin`.

3. Add an entry to set the classpath variable pointing to the directory containing the `log4j.properties` file. For example, in the following configuration:

   ```
   set CP=%CP%;C:\Jakarta-tomcat-3.2.1\webapps\logdemo\
   ```

   we would add an entry to the `tomcat.bat` file as follows:

   ```
   set TOMCAT_OPTS=-Dlog4j.configuration=log4j.properties
   ```

4. Start up Tomcat, and it will load the `log4j.properties` file and use it to print log4j logging information.

Configuring Through the Servlet Initialization

You can configure Apache log4j at initialization of the servlet by passing it the name of the properties file through the application-specific `web.xml` file.

1. Go to the `logdemo/WEB-INF` folder of Tomcat.

2. Open the `web.xml` file and enter the following servlet configuration:

   ```
   <servlet>
     <servlet-name>LoggingServlet</servlet-name>
     <servlet-class>LoggingServlet.class</servlet-class>

     <init-param>
     <param-name>log4j-conf</param-name>
     <param-value>log4j.properties</param-value>
     </init-param>

     <load-on-startup>1</load-on-startup>
   </servlet>
   ```

3. Override the init method in the LoggingServlet (Listing 2-5) as follows:

```
public void init()throws ServletException
{
    super.init();
    String configFile = getInitParameter("log4j-conf");
    PropertyConfigurator.configureAndWatch(configFile);
}
```

4. Start up Tomcat, and the LoggingServlet will configure it through the log4j.properties file.

An Example Servlet

One of the most frequently encountered server-based deployment environments is the Web server and servlet environment. Listing 2-5, LoggingServlet.java, shows a simple servlet to demonstrate the use of log4j within the Web server environment.

▓**Note** To compile the Java servlet program, you need a 1.x version of servlet.jar in your classpath. If you are using Tomcat as explained in this example, you will find servlet.jar in the /lib directory of the Tomcat installation.

Listing 2-5. *LoggingServlet.java*

```
import javax.servlet.*;
import javax.servlet.http.*;
import java.io.PrintWriter;
import java.io.IOException;
import org.apache.log4j.*;

public class LoggingServlet extends HttpServlet {
    private static Logger logger =
Logger.getLogger(LoggingServlet.class);

 public void init()throws ServletException
 {
            super.init();
            String configFile = getInitParameter("log4j-conf");
            PropertyConfigurator.configureAndWatch(configFile);
}

    public void doPost(HttpServletRequest req, HttpServletResponse res)
                    throws IOException, ServletException
    {
        logger.info("invoked the LoggingServlet...");
        PrintWriter writer = res.getWriter();
        writer.println("Check your web server console...");
```

```
        writer.flush();
        writer.close();
    }

}
```

Next, we will write a small HTML file to invoke this servlet:

```
<html>
<body>
<h1>Please enter value and press submit</h1>
<form method="POST"
action="http://localhost:8080/logdemo/servlet/LoggingServlet">
<input type=submit value=Invoke>
</body>
</html>
```

Notice that the form named "action" is pointing to the LoggingServlet, which is executed in a host named localhost that listens to port 8080. This is the default port for the HTTP request.

We override the init() method of the servlet to initialize log4j. We also use the configureAndWatch() method of the PropertyConfigurator class. This makes sure that the config file log4j.properties is watched every 60 seconds (set as the default value within the PropertyConfigurator class) and anytime the configuration file is modified, log4j will automatically reinitialize itself with the changed values.

Within the servlet we obtain a Logger instance, and within the doPost() method we use the Logger.info() method to print the logging information.

Once we invoke the LoggingServlet from the HTML page, we can see the following output in the Tomcat console:

```
invoked the LoggingServlet...
```

▓**Note** We can redirect logging information anywhere we would like to by changing the log4j configuration file.

You are now familiar with the various aspects of configuring log4j. Starting with the next section, we will explore different log4j objects in detail.

Level Object

The org.apache.log4j.Level object replaces the org.apache.log4j.Priority object in previous versions of log4j. It denotes the priority or severity associated with a logging message. A Logger and Appender can have threshold levels associated with them. Logging messages get filtered according to how their levels compare to those of both the Logger and Appender objects. Hence, it is possible to turn off or on a certain level of logging by changing the levels associated with the Logger and these objects. The Level class defines the following levels:

- ALL *(lowest)*: This level has the lowest possible rank and prints all logging information.

- DEBUG: This level prints debugging information helpful in the development stage.

- INFO: This level prints informational messages that help determine the flow of control within an application.

- WARN: This level prints information related to some faulty and unexpected behavior of the system that needs immediate attention to forestall application malfunction.

- ERROR: This level prints error-related messages.

- FATAL: This level prints system-critical information about problems that are causing the application to crash.

- OFF *(highest)*: This is the highest level, and it turns off printing for all the logging information.

The levels have unique integer values attached to them and are arranged in the preceding list from lowest to highest value.

Logger Object

The Logger object is the main object that an application developer uses to log any message. Once the logging information is passed to a logger, the rest is done behind the scenes. Logger objects only encapsulate logging messages and do not have any knowledge about the destination or the formatting of those messages. This is where the Appender and Layout objects come into the picture, as we will see in Chapters 3 and 4.

The Logger objects acting within a particular instance of an application follow a parent-child hierarchy. To illustrate this concept, consider Figure 2-2.

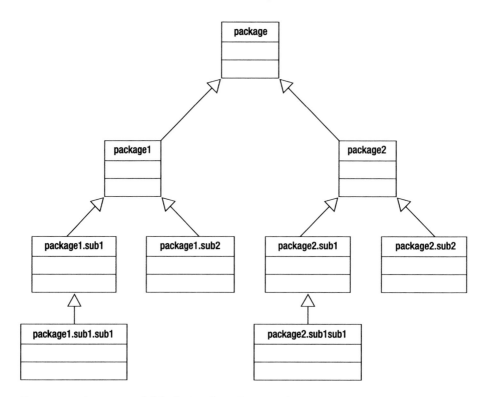

Figure 2-2. *The parent-child relationship of Logger objects*

At the top of the hierarchy exists a root logger. The root logger exists outside the scope of any custom logger hierarchy that we may come up with. It always exists as the root logger for all possible logger hierarchies, and it has no namespace. All the other application-specific Logger objects are child objects to the root logger. The parent-child relationship of loggers signifies the dependency of the loggers acting within the same application. A child logger can inherit properties from its parent logger recursively up the tree. Typically, a child logger will inherit the following properties from its parent logger(s):

- Level: If the child logger has no explicit tree level specified, it will use the level of its closest parent or the first proper level it finds recursively up the hierarchy.

- Appender: If there is no appender attached to a logger, the child logger uses the appender of its closest parent logger or the first appender it finds recursively up the tree.

- ResourceBundle: ResourceBundles are key-value pattern properties files used for the localization of logging messages. A child logger inherits any ResourceBundle associated with its parent logger.

This hierarchical relationship also means that when a child logger is using the properties of its parent logger, any change to the parent's properties will affect the child's behavior. Changes to properties of child loggers, on the other hand, do not affect parent loggers. The additivity property dictates this parent-child relationship in the context of log4j.

By default, Logger objects have the additivity flag set to true. You can disable the additivity property for a child logger by setting the additivity flag to false, in which case the child will not inherit any of the parent logger's properties. The additivity property is controlled by the following method in the Logger object:

```
public boolean setAdditivity(boolean value)
```

or by setting the configuration as

```
log4j.logger.loggerName.additivity=false
```

How to Obtain a Logger

We can use various methods in the Logger class to create new named loggers, obtain an existing named logger, and log messages at various levels of priority. The Logger class does not allow us to instantiate a new Logger instance; rather it provides two static methods for obtaining a Logger object instance:

```
public static Logger getRootLogger();
public static Logger getLogger(String name);
```

The first of the two methods returns the application instance's root logger. As I mentioned earlier, the root logger always exists and does not have a name. Any other named Logger object instance is obtained through the second method by passing the name of the logger. The name of the logger can be any arbitrary string. To make application logging more effective and self-explanatory, the naming of loggers plays an important role. Generally speaking, you should give a Logger object a name corresponding to the package it belongs to or a fully qualified class name from which the Logger instance is created. This name can be strongly typed as a string containing the name of the package or the class. But a more flexible way of naming the Logger is depicted in the following example (which was also presented in Listing 2-4):

```
Logger logger = Logger.getLogger(SimpleLogging.class.getPackage().getName());
```

This approach is refactoring proof; if for any reason we decide to change the package structure, the logging code need not change. You can see the benefit of this approach, as opposed to strongly typing the logger name, which is unlikely to render much benefit to the application.

Note *Refactoring* is the process of improving the internal design of the code without affecting the external behavior of the code.

When a new Logger instance is created, the LogManager stores the instance in namespace storage with the namespace as the key. If we try to create the same Logger instance again while the application is running, the existing instance is returned. In a real-life application, we would probably *not* use the root logger, but instead obtain our own named loggers. All the named loggers by default inherit the properties from the root logger recursively.

Logging Information

Once we obtain an instance of a named logger, we can use several methods of the logger to log messages. The Logger class has the following methods for printing the logging information. We have to remember that the Logger class inherits all these methods from the previous Category class. The methods inherited from the Category class will sometimes refer to another historic class, Priority, which is now replaced by the Level class. We can interchange the use of Category with Logger, and Priority with Level without affecting the application's integrity.

Note As the Logger object has replaced the Category object, so too have some methods in the Category object been deprecated. We have to be cautious in using those methods and possibly avoid using any method directly from the Category class. In version 1.3 of log4j, the Category class will be removed.

Level-Based Logging Methods

The methods listed in Table 2-2 are level-based logging methods. Each method assigns a particular level to the message being logged.

Table 2-2. *Logging Methods in the Logger Class*

Method	Description
public void debug(Object message);	This method prints messages with the level Level.DEBUG.
public void error(Object message);	This method prints messages with the level Level.ERROR.
public void fatal(Object message);	This method prints messages with the level Level.FATAL.
public void info(Object message);	This method prints messages with the level Level.INFO.
public void warn(Object message);	This method prints messages with the level Level.WARN.

A similar set of methods exists with the logging message and an instance of the java.lang. Throwable object. The Throwable object denotes the error condition that should be logged and contains the stack trace of the application. The Throwable instance can be null. This set of methods taking a Throwable object instance helps us log any particularly erroneous situation arising within the application, and the stack trace enables us to determine the exact location of the error.

Logging in Multiple Languages

One thing that makes the Java language so flexible is its localization feature. Apache log4j uses this feature to publish localized logging messages, which means application logging becomes language independent. This localization is done through a java.util.ResourceBundle object and by attaching separate locale-specific message properties files to the application.

The java.util.ResourceBundle is a technique to make our program language independent. With this technique at the simplest level, we use certain keys within our program. These keys map to certain messages (values) and are defined within a properties file. The ResourceBundle properties files are locale specific. For example, we can define messages in English and German in two separate properties files named MyResources_en.properties and MyResources_de.properties. In the program we can use the ResourceBundle object with the name MyResource.properties. In a situation where the locale requires German, our program will automatically pick up the resource named MyResources_de.properties.

The ResourceBundle is specified by invoking the method Logger.setResourceBundle (ResourceBundle name). It can also be set via the configuration file as follows:

```
log4j.logger.loggerName.resourceBundle=resourceBundle name
```

The ResourceBundle loads the locale-specific properties file containing the message key and the localized message value, which the application uses to publish messages. The Logger class provides the following methods for localized logging, which accept the Priority or Level object of the logging message, the localization key, and a Throwable instance:

```
public void l7dlog(Priority p, String key, Throwable t);
public void l7dlog(Priority p, String key, Object params[], Throwable t);
```

The first method is a straightforward one. It looks for the localized message with "key" as the localization key. If the key cannot fetch any value from the ResourceBundle, then the key itself is used as the message string. The second method accepts an array of Object, which contains all the parameters to be localized. The formatting pattern that matches the key is obtained, and all the parameters passed in the array are localized using the java.text.MessageFormat. format(String, Object[]) method.

Generic Logging

The Logger class allows us to use generic logging methods for situations in which the level of logging is not predefined. The following are generic logging methods:

```
public void log(Priority p, Object message);
public void log(Priority p, Object message, Throwable t);
public void log(String fqcn, Priority p, Object message, Throwable t);
```

The first two methods are obvious in the sense that they accept the logging level and the message object as the argument, and optionally accept a java.lang.Throwable instance. The last method is the most generic one, and it takes an extra argument, fqcn, which is the fully qualified name of the caller class. The generic logging methods are rarely used directly from an application. But any wrapper class in the Logger class may use these generic methods internally to print logging information.

All the preceding methods accept as a parameter a java.lang.Object, which is the message to be printed. This can represent any arbitrary object. The Logger object passes this object to the associated Appender object(s), and Appender objects in turn pass the message to the Layout objects. The Layout objects will interpret the object and render it into a human-readable format. I will discuss this process with the help of org.apache.log4j.or.ObjectRenderer in Chapter 5.

Configuration Methods

The Logger class offers a couple of methods to configure the Logger instance. These methods can add or remove Appenders and can set the Level of the Logger instance.

```
public void addAppender(Appender appender)
public void removeAppender(Appender appender)
public void removeAppender(String name)
public void removeAllAppenders()
public void setLevel(Level level)
```

All these methods are self-explanatory, but take care when using them, as they override the default configuration.

▓Caution You should not use these methods to set the configuration information directly, as doing so essentially hard-codes the configuration parameters with the source code. A better approach is to configure the Logger with the external configuration file.

Conditions of Successful Logging

Using the logging methods does not guarantee that logging information will be published. Logging information is filtered through various layers before it gets printed to a preferred destination, as you may recall from the "Overview of the log4j Architecture" section. For a logging call to be successful, the following conditions must be satisfied.

- Any logging information will be approved by a logger if and only if the level p associated with the logging message is equal to or greater than the level q assigned to the logger. In other words, if $p >= q$ is satisfied, the logger will approve the message and pass it on to the associated Appender objects.

- The Appender objects, in turn, can have Filter objects associated with them. If they do, the Filter objects need to approve the logging messages in order to publish them to their final destination.

- Finally, if you are using any specialized Layout or ObjectRenderer objects, they all need to be successful in order to publish the logging messages.

With respect to Logger, the main filtering happens at the logging levels. As discussed earlier, a Logger will have its own Level or will inherit the Level of its closest parent in the hierarchy recursively. Thus, if a Logger has a default Level of WARN, any attempt to do logging with the info() method will produce no logging information.

A Logger Example

Listing 2-6, LoggerDemo.java, demonstrates the basic logging methods and experiment with localizing the logging information.

Listing 2-6. *LoggerDemo.java*

```java
package com.apress.logging.log4j;

import org.apache.log4j.*;

/** This class demonstrates the basic use of Logger class methods
 */
public class LoggerDemo {

    private static Logger logger =
Logger.getLogger(LoggerDemo.class.getPackage().getName());

    /** Creates a new instance of LoggerDemo */
    public LoggerDemo(String rbName) {
        //setting the use of parent handler to false
        logger.setAdditivity(false);
        logger.debug("Set the parent additivity to false...");
        logger.setResourceBundle(java.util.ResourceBundle.getBundle(rbName));
        logger.debug("Set the resource bundle...");

    }

    /** demonstrates the basic level based logging methods
     * @param name name to say hello to
     */
    public void doLogging(String name) {
        logger.debug("Entered the doLogging method..");
        String str = "Hello ";
        String output = null;

        if(name == null) {
            output = "Anonymous";
            logger.warn("No name passed, set to anonymous...");
        }else {
            output = str.concat(name);
            logger.info("Constructed the string object..."+output);
        }

        logger.info("printing the message...");
        logger.debug("Exiting the doLogging method...");
    }
```

```
/** demonstrates the localized logging methods
 */
public void doLocalizedLogging() {

    logger.l7dlog(Level.DEBUG, "Entry", null);
    logger.l7dlog(Level.DEBUG, "Exit", null);
}

public static void main(String args[]) {
    String name = args[0];
    String rbName = args[1];
    LoggerDemo demo = new LoggerDemo(rbName);
    demo.doLogging(name);
    demo.doLocalizedLogging();
}
}
```

To execute this program, we use the log4j.properties file described in Listing 2-3. What follows are the steps for a successful logging in this example.

1. First, we obtain a Logger instance with the package name of the LoggerDemo class as a class variable.

2. In the constructor, we set the additivity property of this logger to false, which means that this logger will not forward any logging requests to its immediate parent logger.

3. Next, we set the ResourceBundle for this logger, which will be used to localize the logging information.

4. The doLogging() method uses several logging methods from the Logger class. Logging information with less severity is printed with the debug() method, and other important messages are printed with the info() and warn() methods of the Logger class.

5. The doLocalizedLogging() method simply prints two messages to demonstrate how a message passed to the logging methods is interpreted as the localization key and the corresponding message value is printed.

Consider the logging_fr.properties file containing the localization key and value:

```
Entry=Entrer
Exit=Sortir
```

When the l7dlog() method is called by passing the messages "Entry" and "Exit" respectively, the log4j framework looks into logging_fr.properties and prints the corresponding values as the logging information.

If we execute the program with the following command:

```
java -Dlog4j.configuration=log4j.properties
com.apress.logging.log4j.LoggerDemo sam logging_fr
```

we will see the following information being printed in the console:

```
DEBUG - Set the parent additivity to false...
DEBUG - Set the resource bundle...
DEBUG - Entered the doLogging method..
INFO - Constructed the string object...Hello sam
INFO - printing the message...
DEBUG - Exiting the doLogging method...
DEBUG - Entrer
DEBUG - Sortir
```

Notice that the last two lines of the logging message are printed as localized messages. The information with the level DEBUG is intended to be printed only during development to provide a better understanding of the control flow of the application. We can easily turn off DEBUG-level messages by changing the level in the log4j.properties file as follows:

```
log4j.logger.com.apress.logging.log4j=INFO,testAppender
```

With the new level set to INFO, the logger will print only messages with a priority equal to or greater than INFO. If we reexecute the program with the preceding settings, we will see the following output to the console:

```
INFO - Constructed the string object...Hello sam
INFO - printing the message...
```

Notice that DEBUG-level messages are omitted this time.

LogManager Object

The org.apache.log4j.LogManager class manages the creation and storage of each named logger created from within an application. Internally it uses another helper class, org.apache.log4j. Hierarchy, to store the reference of each Logger object created. The hierarchy is such that every child logger created will have a pointer to its parent logger, but a parent logger will not have any reference to its child logger. Also, log4j does not restrict application developers from instantiating a child logger before its parent. In such scenarios, the child logger instance is created, and in the Hierarchy class it is stored with an empty node for the future assignment of a parent logger whenever it is created.

Application developers normally do not have to use the Hierarchy class. Instead, they use the convenience methods that the LogManager and Logger classes provide to create and obtain any named logger. Note that when we change the property of any existing named logger, a new instance is never created. The existing reference is obtained from the Hierarchy class, and the properties are changed to that reference. This is the reason why methods in the Logger class such as

```
public void addAppender(Appender appender)
```

are synchronized to make sure that two threads do not operate on the same instance of a named logger at the same time.

The LogManager class provides the useful methods described in Table 2-3.

Table 2-3. *Methods in the LogManager Class*

Method	Description
public static Enumeration getCurrentLoggers();	This method returns an enumeration of the existing named loggers.
public static Logger exists(String name);	This method checks for the existence of a particular named logger.
public static Logger getLogger(String name);	This method obtains an existing named logger.

In the next section, we will explore the other aspects of log4j that help us deal with client-specific logging information.

Nested Diagnostic Context (NDC)

Logging is most useful in complex distributed applications. The majority of real-life complex distributed systems are multithreaded. A good example of such is a Web application written with Java servlet technology. Each servlet handles multiple clients at the same time, yet the logging code written within the servlet is the same. It is almost always required that the logging output of one client be differentiated from another. One approach is to execute a different logging thread per client. But this solution may not always be ideal. A less complex approach may be to uniquely stamp each logging output with some client-specific information. This is where the *Nested Diagnostic Context* (NDC) comes into the picture.

The NDC class in log4j uses the methods listed in Table 2-4 to manage the information in the NDC stack.

Table 2-4. *Methods in the NDC Class*

Method	Description
public static void pop();	This method is called when exiting a context.
public static void push(String message);	This method adds the diagnostic context for the current thread.
public static void remove();	This method is called when exiting a thread. It removes the diagnostic context for the particular thread.

Notice that all the methods in the NDC class are static. The NDC is managed per thread as a stack of contextual information. It is important to make sure that NDC's remove() method is called when leaving the run() method of a thread. This ensures the thread's garbage collection. Interestingly, a thread can inherit the NDC from another thread by calling the inherit(Stack stack) method of the NDC class. This is very useful when we want to compare the contextual information of two different threads.

Message Diagnostic Context (MDC)

The *Message Diagnostic Context* (MDC) is a mechanism to store client-specific data using the java.util.Map format. The key of this Map can be replaced by its value in the conversion pattern specified with the Layout object used with an appender. The MDC class provides the methods in Table 2-5 to manipulate the key and the value stored within the Map.

Table 2-5. *Methods in the MDC Class*

Method	Description
`public static Object get(String key);`	This method retrieves the `Object` stored against the key.
`public static void put(String key, Object o);`	This method stores the `Object` o against the key.
`public static void remove(String key)`	This method removes the mapping of any `Object` with the key.

The following illustrates the concepts associated with the MDC and NDC objects in a much clearer way. Imagine that we have a Java servlet program that is multithreaded and handles multiple clients at the same time. We might wish to stamp each logging output with some client-specific information such as the client's IP address. Let's modify the LoggingServlet.java (shown in Listing 2-5) to use MDC and NDC to separate each logging output for each client request. To start, insert the following code inside the doPost() method:

```
public void doPost(HttpServletRequest req, HttpServletResponse res)
                  throws IOException, ServletException
{
    String remoteAddress = req.getRemoteAddr();
    String remoteHost = req.getRemoteHost();

    //pushing to NDC
    NDC.push(remoteHost);
    //mapping in MDC
    MDC.put("remoteAddress", remoteAddress);
    logger.info("invoked the LoggingServlet...");
    PrintWriter writer = res.getWriter();
    writer.println("Check your web server console...");
    writer.flush();
    writer.close();
}
```

In the preceding piece of code, we obtain the remote host name (in the NDC) and the remote host address (in the MDC). Now we will modify the log4j.properties file as follows to change the conversion pattern used by the appender to display the MDC and NDC information:

```
log4j.appender.testAppender.layout.conversionPattern=%x -%X{remoteAddress} %m%n
```

The %x displays the NDC information and %X{variable name} displays the MDC information. Note that the variable name specified within the MDC pattern has to match the variable name assigned within the code. Now the logging output will contain the NDC and MDC information as follows:

```
hostname1 - host address1 invoked the LoggingServlet...
hostname2 - host address2 invoked the LoggingServlet...
```

It is evident how useful the NDC and MDC information can be in distinguishing the logging output although the same information is being printed.

Conclusion

In this chapter, we have examined the various key objects in the log4j framework and explored how these objects interact to capture, filter, and produce logging information to various destinations. Besides the key objects, log4j involves many auxiliary objects that help handle the logging information. In the next chapter, you will learn about different Appender objects in log4j.

CHAPTER 3

■ ■ ■

Destination of Logging—The Appender Objects

In the previous chapter, you learned about the Logger objects and examined the capabilities of log4j. The ability to filter logging information and use different methods in the Logger class is a great feature for application developers. But the Logger itself is not capable of printing logging messages. It does so with the help of Appender objects. Appender objects are primarily responsible for printing logging messages to different destinations such as consoles, files, sockets, NT event logs, etc. Occasionally, Appender objects can have Filter objects associated with them to make further decisions about the logging of a particular message.

The writing of information to the preferred destination attached to any particular Appender can be synchronous or asynchronous depending on how the application developer uses the Appender. It is a major benefit that Appender objects are quite flexible in terms of destination of the logging information. It is possible to create Appender objects to write to a database and JMS to achieve a distributed logging framework. In this chapter, we will discuss the different Appender objects available in log4j. The class diagram in Figure 3-1 depicts the relationship of Appender objects and how they are organized.

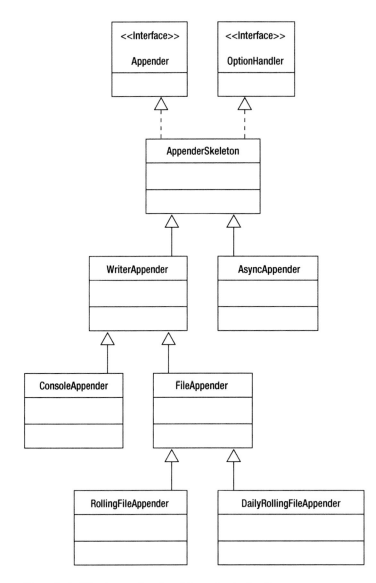

Figure 3-1. *The Appender class hierarchy in log4j*

Properties of Appender

Each Appender object has different properties associated with it, and these properties indicate the behavior of that object. In general, Appender objects will have the properties listed in Table 3-1.

Table 3-1. *Properties of Appender*

Property	Description
layout	Each Appender object needs to know how to format the logging information passed to it. It uses the Layout objects and the conversion pattern associated with them to format the logging information.
target	Each Appender object will have a target destination attached to it. The target may be a console, a file, or another item depending on the appender.
level	Each Appender object can have a threshold Level associated with it. Logging information is compared with the threshold level, and if the logging request level is equal to or greater than this threshold, the logging information is processed further; otherwise it is ignored.
threshold	Each Appender can have a threshold level associated with it independent of the logger level. The Appender ignores any logging messages that have a level lower than the threshold level.
filter	It is possible to attach Filter objects to Appenders. The Filter objects can analyze logging information beyond level matching and decide whether logging requests should be handled by a particular Appender or ignored.

Depending on the type of Appender object, each Appender can have other special attributes. We will discuss each Appender object in upcoming sections, but first we will take a look at adding Appender objects to Logger objects.

Adding Appenders to Loggers

Logger objects require one or more Appender objects to be associated with them in order to print logging information to a particular destination. We can add an Appender object to a Logger by including the following setting in the configuration file with the following method:

```
log4j.logger.[logger-name]=level, appender1,appender..n
```

In the XML configuration format, the same configuration will look like this:

```
<logger name="com.apress.logging.log4j" additivity="false">
    <appender-ref ref="appender1"/>
    <appender-ref ref="appender2"/>
</logger>
```

Or we can add an Appender to a Logger programmatically by using the following method in the Logger class:

```
public void addAppender(Appender appender);
```

The addAppender() method adds an Appender to the Logger object. As the example configuration demonstrates, it is possible to add many Appender objects to a logger in a comma-separated list, each printing logging information to separate destinations. But note that Appenders are additive. Each logging request to a logger will be forwarded to all the Appender objects associated with it, and also to all the Appender objects associated with its parent loggers in the hierarchy.

You can turn the additivity feature off by setting the additivity flag to false by calling the setAdditivity(Boolean value) (see the "Logger Object" section of Chapter 2). If the additivity flag is set to false, the logging information will be forwarded only to the Appender objects associated with a particular Logger object.

Tip Although appenders can be added to loggers programmatically, a better approach is to use the configuration file. Having configurable properties for logging behavior is more flexible and requires no change of source code to get a completely different logging behavior; you can achieve that result by merely changing the configuration file.

Logger-to-Appender Collaboration

So far we have seen how Logger objects encapsulate logging information and how different Appender objects are capable of printing logging information to different destinations. But how do Logger objects pass logging information to Appender objects? Creating an intermediate link object named LoggingEvent does the trick.

1. The org.apache.log4j.spi.LoggingEvent class encapsulates all the relevant logging information such as the fully qualified name of the caller class, the level of the logging message, the message itself, the Logger instance, the timestamp, and optionally a java.lang.Throwable instance.

2. Before proceeding to hand over the logging request to any associated Appender, the Logger creates an instance of the LoggingEvent object with the logging-related information.

3. The Logger object then calls the doAppend(LoggingEvent event) method of the Appender objects.

4. The doAppend() method performs some crucial checks on the logging request such as comparing the requested logging level with the threshold level of any Appender associated with the Logger, checking if the Appender is open, and checking any associated Filter object with the Appender.

5. If it finds a Filter object, it invokes that Filter object to make further decisions about the logging request. Once approved, the append() method of the associated subclass Appender object takes over and publishes the logging information.

Thread-Safety in log4j

The doAppend() method in each of the Appender objects is synchronized. This means log4j is thread-safe and publishing of logging events happens in a synchronous manner. On the other hand, log4j is designed to work with multiple threads acting together.

WriterAppender

WriterAppender is a high-level Appender object that extends the org.apache.log4j.AppenderSkeleton object. WriterAppender writes logging information to one of the following, depending on whether the application developer has set the target to either a Writer object or an OutputStream object:

- A java.io.Writer object

- A java.io.OutputStream object

The WriterAppender class can have the following properties:

Properties of WriterAppender

Table 3-2 presents the configurable properties available to WriterAppender. Note that these properties can be configured either through a configuration file or programmatically.

Table 3-2. *Configurable Properties of WriterAppender*

Property	Description
immediateFlush	This property indicates if the output stream should be flushed each time there is a request to write certain logging information. By default, this option is set to true. If the flag is set to false, then the underlying stream can defer the writing of logging information to physical media to a later time.
encoding	It is possible to use any encoding scheme for writing logging information. By default, WriterAppender uses the system-specific encoding scheme.
threshold	This denotes the cutoff level of logging for WriterAppender. Any logging request that has a level below this level will be ignored. There is no threshold level set as default, which means that level filtering is not active for this Appender object.
target	This specifies any java.io.Writer object or java.io.OutputStream object.

Note Flushing the stream for every logging request is costly and can slow up performance by 10 to 20 percent, but it guarantees that all the information is logged. If the immediateFlush property is set to false, then there is chance that some logging information will be missing if there is an arbitrary exit from the application or if the application crashes.

The principal method in the WriterAppender class is

```
public void append(LoggingEvent event);
```

This serves as the entry point for this WriterAppender. Whenever a logging request is made via the append() method, the following process takes place:

1. It invokes the protected boolean checkEntryConditions() method to check if the conditions for logging are valid.

2. It checks if there is a set output target and a layout attached to it.

3. If these conditions are not met, the writing operation returns and prints the appropriate error message to the console.

   Remember that threshold-level checking and any filtering of the logging request through any of the associated Filter objects has already been done by the base class, AppenderSkeleton, before the request is delegated to any particular Appender object.

4. Otherwise, if everything is appropriate, it proceeds to write the logging information to the associated target.

Variations of WriterAppender

WriterAppender has two subclasses, ConsoleAppender and FileAppender, which write to a console and any file object, respectively. In real life, we will hardly use WriterAppender directly. Instead, we will use one of the subclasses, as described next.

ConsoleAppender

org.apache.log4j.ConsoleAppender is a very simple class designed to write logging information to either System.out or System.err. The destination of the log messages can be configured via a property named target. This class extends the org.apache.log4j.WriterAppender class. Any logging application intended to print logging information to a console should use this ConsoleAppender. Interestingly, it overrides the closeWriter() method from its superclass, WriterAppender, and does nothing, as the console stream should not be closed.

Properties of ConsoleAppender

The configurable properties of ConsoleAppender are described in Table 3-3.

Table 3-3. *Configurable Properties of ConsoleAppender*

Property	Description
immediateFlush	This flag is by default set to true, which results in the console stream being flushed with each logging output request.
encoding	It is possible to use any character-encoding scheme, but the default is the platform-specific encoding scheme.
threshold	This is the cutoff logging level. Any logging request with a level below the threshold will be ignored. There is no default threshold level specified.
target	The target destination of the logging output—either System.out or System.err. The default is System.out.

A ConsoleAppender Example

Listing 3-1 presents a sample log4j configuration file with ConsoleAppender.

Listing 3-1. *ConsoleAppender Configuration*

```
log4j.rootCategory=debug,console
log4j.logger.com.apress.logging.log4j=debug,console
log4j.additivity.com.apress.logging.log4j=false

log4j.appender.console=org.apache.log4j.ConsoleAppender
#try assigning the destination to be error stream
log4j.appender.console.target=System.err

#set a layout for the console appender and set the conversion pattern
log4j.appender.console.layout=org.apache.log4j.PatternLayout
log4j.appender.console.layout.conversionPattern=%m%n
```

Listing 3-2 presents a similar configuration in XML style.

Listing 3-2. *ConsoleAppender Configuration—XML Style*

```xml
<?xml version="1.0" encoding="UTF-8" ?>
<!DOCTYPE log4j:configuration SYSTEM "log4j.dtd">
<log4j:configuration>
<appender name="dataAccessLogger" class="org.apache.log4j.ConsoleAppender">
   <param name="target" value="System.err"/>
    <layout class="org.apache.log4j.PatternLayout">
        <param name="conversionPattern" value="%m%n"/>
   </layout>
  </appender>

<logger name="com.apress.logging.log4j">
   <level value="debug"/>
   <appender-ref ref="dataAccessLogger"/>
</logger>
  <root>
    <priority value ="debug" />
    <appender-ref ref="dataAccessLogger"/>
  </root>

</log4j:configuration>
```

FileAppender

org.apache.log4j.FileAppender extends the org.apache.log4j.WriterAppender class and writes logging information to a file. FileAppender is flexible in terms of how information should be logged to the destination file. It can enable buffered writing, append or overwrite information to the same file, and roll (create a new file) the filenames depending on data and time. FileAppender is often the most used appender in real-life applications. The rich features available in different flavors of FileAppender meet all needs for maintaining the logging information.

Properties of FileAppender

Table 3-4 presents all the configurable parameters of FileAppender.

Table 3-4. *Properties of FileAppender*

Properties	Description	Default
immediateFlush	This flag is by default set to true, which results in the output stream to the file being flushed with each append operation.	true
encoding	It is possible to use any character-encoding scheme, but the default is the platform-specific encoding scheme.	None
threshold	The threshold level for this appender.	None

Continued

Table 3-4. *Continued*

Properties	Description	Default
Filename	The name of the file to which the logging information will be written. The filename can be specified with a UNIX-style variable name such as ${user.home}/log.out, which means the location of the file log.out should be in the system-specific user.home directory.	None
fileAppend	This is by default set to true, which results in the logging information being appended to the end of the same file.	true
bufferedIO	This flag indicates whether we need buffered writing enabled.	false
bufferSize	If bufferedI/O is enabled, this indicates the buffer size.	8KB

Writing the Message Quietly

FileAppender delegates the printing of logging information to its superclass, WriterAppender. Interestingly, it sets the Writer object of WriterAppender to a custom writer, org.apache.log4j. helpers.QuietWriter. The QuietWriter is a normal java.io.Writer except that it does not throw any exception if there is a problem in I/O operation. Instead, it passes the problem to an org.apache. log4j.spi.ErrorHandler object. The ErrorHandler is declared as an interface; one concrete implementation of this interface is org.apache.log4j.helpers.OnlyOnceErrorHandler. The OnlyOnceErrorHandler logs only the first error message to System.err and silently ignores the rest. This is helpful to avoid flooding the logging destination with error messages.

Sample Configuration of FileAppender

You can set the configuration parameters of the FileAppender class via the methods inherited from the AppenderSkeleton class. However, this ties up the code with the configuration information. I recommend that you separate the configuration information from the source code and specify this information through the configuration file settings. Listing 3-3 represents a sample FileAppender configuration.

Listing 3-3. *Sample FileAppender Configuration—Properties Style*

```
log4j.logger.com.apress.logging.log4j=debug,dest
log4j.additivity.com.apress.logging.log4j=false

log4j.appender.dest = org.apache.log4j.FileAppender
#set the name of the file
log4j.appender.dest.File=${user.home}/log.out

#setting the immediate flush to true (default)
log4j.appender.dest.ImmediateFlush=true

#setting the threshold
log4j.appender.dest.Threshold=debug
```

```
#setting the append to false, overwrite
log4j.appender.dest.Append=false

#set a layout for the appender
log4j.appender.dest.layout=org.apache.log4j.PatternLayout
log4j.appender.dest.layout.conversionPattern=%m%n
```

Listing 3-4 presents the same configuration in XML style.

Listing 3-4. *Sample FileAppender Configuration—XML Style*

```xml
<?xml version="1.0" encoding="UTF-8" ?>
<!DOCTYPE log4j:configuration SYSTEM "log4j.dtd">
<log4j:configuration>
<appender name="dest" class="org.apache.log4j.FileAppender">
   <param name="file" value="${user.home}/log.out"/>
   <param name="threshold" value="debug"/>
   <param name="immediateFlush" value="true"/>
   <param name="append" value="false"/>

  <layout class="org.apache.log4j.PatternLayout">
        <param name="conversionPattern" value="%m%n"/>
  </layout>
  </appender>

<logger name="com.apress.logging.log4j" additivity="false">
   <level value="debug"/>
   <appender-ref ref="dest"/>
</logger>

</log4j:configuration>
```

This configuration file configures an appender named dest. The appender dest is set to be a FileAppender object. The configuration file sets different properties for this FileAppender object. Note how I specify the destination filename using UNIX-style variable substitution.

Rolling in Multiple Files—RollingFileAppender

Logging all the messages into one file would make the logging file grow enormously with time. It would become difficult to find anything in that file and would create the risk of corruption. The solution is to distribute logging information to multiple files. org.apache.log4j. RollingFileAppender helps achieve this. This class extends the FileAppender class. It writes the log information to a specified file, but writes, or *rolls over*, to a secondary file when the primary file reaches a certain size. The RollingFileAppender has the properties described in the following section, in addition to all the properties inherited from the FileAppender class.

Properties of RollingFileAppender

Table 3-5 presents the configuration parameters specific to RollingFileAppender in addition to the FileAppender.

Table 3-5. *Configuration Properties of RollingFileAppender*

Properties	Description	Default
maxFileSize	This is the critical size of the file above which the file will be rolled.	10MB
maxBackupIndex	This property denotes the number of backup files to be created.	1

Useful Operations in RollingFileAppender

The RollingFileAppender class has several useful methods to control its behavior, and these appear in Table 3-6.

Table 3-6. *Methods in the RollingFileAppender Class*

Method	Description
public void rollOver()	This method performs the usual rollover operation, which is activated when the maximum file size is reached. Alternatively, the application developer can force the rollover at any stage of the operation. When called, if the maxBackupIndex is >0, then the file log.1 is renamed log.2 and so on for keeping backups. The log.1 file is then closed, and a new file, log.2, is opened to log the next bit of information. If the maxBackupIndex = 0; then the log file is truncated as soon as the maximum file size is reached, and no backup file is created.
public void setMaxBackupIndex(int maxBackupIndex)	This method, which takes a positive value, sets the maximum backup index after which the oldest backup file will be erased. If set to 0, no backup file will be created.
public void setMaxFileSize(long size)	This method is the same as the previous method, except it accepts the file size as a long value.
public void setMaxFileSize(String size)	This method takes the maximum file size after which the file will be rolled over. We can specify the file size with the suffix KB, MB, etc. to indicate kilobytes and megabytes. For example, we can specify a 20-megabyte file size with 20MB.
public void subAppend(LoggingEvent event)	This is the overridden method from the superclass WriterAppender, and it implements the bulk of the writing to a rolling file.

Sample Configuration of RollingFileAppender

Listing 3-5 demonstrates how to configure the RollingFileAppender properties.

Listing 3-5. *Sample RollingFileAppender Configuration—Properties Style*

```
log4j.logger.com.apress.logging.log4j=debug,dest
log4j.additivity.com.apress.logging.log4j=false

#define the appender
log4j.appender.dest = org.apache.log4j.RollingFileAppender

#set the name of the file
log4j.appender.dest.File=${user.home}/log.out

#setting the immediate flush to true (default)
log4j.appender.dest.ImmediateFlush=true

#setting the threshold
log4j.appender.dest.Threshold=ERROR

#setting the append to true, don't overwrite
log4j.appender.dest.Append=true

#set the maximum file size before rollover
log4j.appender.dest.MaxFileSize=10KB

#set the backup index
log4j.appender.dest.MaxBackupIndex=2
```

This configuration file defines a RollingFileAppender named dest. It then sets the other configuration parameters for this appender. This example configuration demonstrates that maximum permissible size of each log file is 10KB. Upon exceeding the maximum size, a new log file will be created (as described in the rollOver() method description). As maxBackupIndex is defined as 2, once the second log file reaches the maximum size, the first log file will be erased and thereafter all the logging information will be rolled back to the first log file. Listing 3-6 demonstrates the same configuration in XML style.

Listing 3-6. *Sample RollingFileAppender Configuration Properties—XML Style*

```
<?xml version="1.0" encoding="UTF-8" ?>
<!DOCTYPE log4j:configuration SYSTEM "log4j.dtd">
<log4j:configuration>
<appender name="dest" class="org.apache.log4j.RollingFileAppender">
   <param name="file" value="${user.home}/log.out"/>
   <param name="threshold" value="error"/>
   <param name="immediateFlush" value="true"/>
   <param name="append" value="true"/>
   <param name="maxFileSize" value="10KB"/>
   <param name="maxBackupIndex" value="2"/>
```

```
    <layout class="org.apache.log4j.PatternLayout">
            <param name="conversionPattern" value="%m%n"/>
    </layout>
    </appender>

<logger name="com.apress.logging.log4j" additivity="false">
    <level value="debug"/>
    <appender-ref ref="dest"/>
</logger>

</log4j:configuration>
```

Rolling the File Daily—DailyRollingFileAppender

Size-based rolling of log files is good for managing a huge amount of logging data and spreading it across multiple files. But in real life, when applications are running day after day, we need to establish a daily logging capacity. The org.apache.log4j.DailyRollingFileAppender object does this for us. It extends the FileAppender class and inherits all its properties. A DatePattern configuration parameter rolls the file. DatePattern indicates when to roll over the file, and the naming convention to be followed. For example, a DailyRollingFileAppender configured with the DatePattern '.' yyyy-MM-dd will end up in log files being renamed as log.out-2002-09-17 on September 17, 2002 at midnight, and the logging will continue to a file named log.out.

DatePattern follows the java.text.SimpleDateFormat object formatting style. You can define the exact date and time of file rolling through DatePattern. Table 3-7 demonstrates how DatePattern controls the rollover schedule, assuming that the log filename is set to log.out.

Table 3-7. *DatePattern Conventions*

DatePattern	Rollover Schedule	Example
'.' yyyy-MM	Roll over at the end of each month and the beginning of the next month.	The log file will be rolled over to log.out-2002-05 on May 31, 2002, and to log.out.2002-09 on September 30, 2002.
'.' yyyy-MM-dd (default)	Roll over at midnight each day.	On September 30, 2002 at midnight, the log.out file will be rolled over to log.out.2002-09-30.
'.' yyyy-MM-dd-a	Roll over at midday and midnight of each day.	On September, 30, 2002 at midday, the log.out file will be rolled over to log.out-2002-09-30-AM, and at midnight that file will be rolled over to log.out.2002-09-30-PM.
'.' yyyy-MM-dd-HH	Roll over at the top of every hour.	On September 30, 2002 at 10:00:000, the log.out file will be rolled over to log.out.2002-09-30-09. Notice that it is prefixed with the previous hour.

DatePattern	Rollover Schedule	Example
`'.' yyyy-MM-dd-HH-mm`	Roll over every minute.	On September 30, 2002 at 10:20:000, the `log.out` file will be rolled over to `log.out.2002-09-30-10-19`.
`'.' yyyy-ww`	Roll over on the first day of each week depending upon the locale.	If the first day of the week is Monday, then at midnight on Sunday, December 28, the `log.out` file will be rolled over to `log.out.2002-52`.

▓**Caution** Do not use ":" anywhere in `DatePattern`. The ":" character is used to specify a protocol, which is not exactly what we want to do with date formats.

As you can see, the `DailyRollingFileAppender` is a very powerful mechanism to obtain fine-grained control over the logging process. In real life, how the logging information is organized is as equally important as which information is logged. The `DailyRollingFileAppender` can prove very helpful in publishing logging information on an hourly, daily, and monthly basis, which helps analyze application performance without your having to deal with too much information or outdated information.

Listing 3-7 demonstrates how to configure a `DailyRollingFileAppender`.

Listing 3-7. *Sample DailyRollingFileAppender Configuration—Properties Style*

```
log4j.logger.com.apress.logging.log4j=debug,dest
log4j.additivity.com.apress.logging.log4j=false

#define the appender
log4j.appender.dest = org.apache.log4j.DailyRollingFileAppender

#set the name of the file
log4j.appender.dest.File=${user.home}/log.out

#setting the immediate flush to true (default)
log4j.appender.dest.ImmediateFlush=true

#setting the threshold
log4j.appender.dest.Threshold=ERROR

#setting the append to false, overwrite
log4j.appender.dest.Append=true

#set the DatePattern
log4j.appender.dest.DatePattern='.' yyyy-MM-dd
```

This configuration file defines the configuration parameters for a `DailyRollingFileAppender` object. The `DatePattern` conversion pattern will follow the convention defined in Table 3-7.

The same configuration file in XML style is presented in Listing 3-8.

Listing 3-8. *Sample DailyRollingFileAppender Configuration—XML Style*

```
<?xml version="1.0" encoding="UTF-8" ?>
<!DOCTYPE log4j:configuration SYSTEM "log4j.dtd">
<log4j:configuration>
<appender name="dest" class="org.apache.log4j.RollingFileAppender">
    <param name="file" value="${user.home}/log.out"/>
    <param name="threshold" value="error"/>
    <param name="immediateFlush" value="true"/>
    <param name="append" value="true"/>
    <param name="datePattern" value=" '.' yyyy-MM-dd "/>

  <layout class="org.apache.log4j.PatternLayout">
        <param name="conversionPattern" value="%m%n"/>
  </layout>
  </appender>

<logger name="com.apress.logging.log4j" additivity="false">
    <level value="debug"/>
    <appender-ref ref="dest"/>
</logger>

</log4j:configuration>
```

A File-Based Logging Example

The program shown later in this section, `FileBasedLoggingDemo.java`, will demonstrate how the different file-based Appender objects handle logging information. You have seen that the file-based Appender objects can write data to a file and roll the logging output file daily or after a specified period. To demonstrate how different files are rolled, the following example shows how to create a thread that will log messages to the file repeatedly. It also shows how to create a configuration file defining all the required logger, appender, and layout information. The properties file `file_logging.properties`, which appears in Listing 3-9, defines the properties required for this file-based logging example.

Listing 3-9. *file_logging.properties*

```
#set the level of the root logger to DEBUG (the lowest level)
#and set its appenders named DEBUG and CONSOLE
log4j.rootLogger = DEBUG, CONSOLE

#set your own logger
log4j.logger.com.apress.logging.log4j=DEBUG, FILE,ROLLING, DAILY

#set the appender CONSOLE
log4j.appender.CONSOLE=org.apache.log4j.ConsoleAppender

#set the appender FILE
log4j.appender.FILE=org.apache.log4j.FileAppender
log4j.appender.FILE.File=${user.home}/out.log
```

```
#set the appender ROLLING
log4j.appender.ROLLING=org.apache.log4j.RollingFileAppender
log4j.appender.ROLLING.File=${user.home}/rolling.log
log4j.appender.ROLLING.MaxFileSize=1KB

#set the appender DAILY
log4j.appender.DAILY=org.apache.log4j.DailyRollingFileAppender
log4j.appender.DAILY.File=${user.home}/daily.log
log4j.appender.DAILY.DatePattern='.' yyyy-MM-dd-HH-mm

#set the layout for the appenders
log4j.appender.CONSOLE.layout=org.apache.log4j.PatternLayout
log4j.appender.CONSOLE.layout.conversionPattern=%p - %m%n

log4j.appender.FILE.layout=org.apache.log4j.PatternLayout
log4j.appender.FILE.layout.conversionPattern=%p - %m%n

log4j.appender.ROLLING.layout=org.apache.log4j.PatternLayout
log4j.appender.ROLLING.layout.conversionPattern=%p - %m%n

log4j.appender.DAILY.layout=org.apache.log4j.PatternLayout
log4j.appender.DAILY.layout.conversionPattern=%p - %m%n
```

The destination files are defined in the configuration file file_logging.properties, and the location of the files is defined by ${user.home}, which means the log files will be created in the user.home system property.

Now that you have seen the properties required for the file-based logging example, take a look at FileBasedLoggingDemo.java, shown in Listing 3-10.

Listing 3-10. *FileBasedLoggingDemo.java*

```java
package com.apress.logging.log4j;

import org.apache.log4j.*;

public class FileBasedLoggingDemo implements Runnable{

    private static Logger logger =
Logger.getLogger(FileBasedLoggingDemo.class.getPackage().getName());
    /** Creates a new instance of FileBasedLoggingDemo */
    public FileBasedLoggingDemo()
    {
    }

    /** This method is called by the application. This method creates
     * a new thread to start logging
```

```java
    */
    public void doLogging()
    {
        Thread t = new Thread(this);
        t.start();
    }


    /** The thread's run() method, which does repeated logging
     * at an interval of 60secs.
     */
    public void run()
    {
        int count=1;
        while(true) {
            //logging information
            try {
                logger.debug("Logging the information..."+count);
                Thread.sleep(60*1000);
                count++;
            }catch(Exception e) {
                logger.warn("Exception occurred", e);
            }
        }
    }
    /** the main method
     */
    public static void main(String args[])
    {
        FileBasedLoggingDemo demo = new FileBasedLoggingDemo();
        demo.doLogging();
    }
}
```

This program will publish logging information to three different files—out.log, rolling.log, and daily.log—through three different appenders—FILE, ROLLING, and DAILY, respectively. The DailyRollingFileAppender is configured to log information and roll at every minute. All the appenders have the append property set to true and will append any logging message to the same file until the rollover criteria is reached. When executed, this program will create files like those shown in the following table in the location defined by the user.home system property.

Filename	Description
daily.log. 2002-09-30-21-35	Logged on September 30, 2002 at 21:35
daily.log. 2002-09-30-21-36	Logged on September 30, 2002 at 21:36
out.log	Normal log file
rolling.log	Initial rolling file
rolling.log.1	Rollover file once the maximum file size is reached

Logging Asynchronously—AsyncAppender

When an application produces a huge amount of logging information, it may be critical to produce logging messages asynchronously, which might improve performance by a considerable amount. As mentioned in the "Thread Safety in log4j" section, the doAppend() method is synchronized. This might reduce performance when thousands of Logger objects are trying to use the same Appender object to print logging information. The AsyncAppender object uses a bounded buffer to store logging events. Once the buffer reaches its size limit, the AsyncAppender dispatches the logging events to specific Appender objects. It is possible to attach multiple Appender objects to AsyncAppender. The AsyncAppender object uses a separate thread for each LoggingEvent object contained in the buffer.

The org.apache.log4j. AysncAppender class extends the org.apache.log4j.AppenderSkeleton class and implements an interface, org.apache.log4j.spi.AppenderAttachable. The interface AppenderAttachable defines a set of methods that any object accepting an Appender object should implement. The set of methods includes those for attaching and removing Appender objects to the class. By default, the AsyncAppender's buffer size can contain 128 LoggingEvent objects. Until release 1.2.6 of log4j, only DOMConfigurator could configure AsyncAppender, through an XML-style configuration file.

Listing 3-11 demonstrates the XML configuration file for AsyncAppender. The configuration defines a ConsoleAppender as the target Appender for the defined AsyncAppender. The ConsoleAppender is given a PatternLayout with a conversion pattern to format the logging message. The named logger com.apress.logging.log4j and the root logger both use the Appender named ASYNC to implement asynchronous logging.

Listing 3-11. *Sample AsyncAppender Configuration—XML Style*

```
<?xml version="1.0" encoding="UTF-8"?>
<!DOCTYPE log4j:configuration SYSTEM "log4j.dtd">

<log4j:configuration xmlns:log4j="http://jakarta.apache.org/log4j/"
debug="true">

 <appender name="ASYNC" class="org.apache.log4j.AsyncAppender">
        <appender-ref ref="CONSOLE"/>
 </appender>

 <appender name="CONSOLE" class="org.apache.log4j.ConsoleAppender">
  <layout class="org.apache.log4j.PatternLayout">
       <param name="ConversionPattern"
                         value="%d %-5p [%t]  - %m%n"/>
  </layout>
 </appender>
     <logger name="com.apress.logging.log4j" additivity="false">
              <level value="debug"/>
              <appender-ref ref="ASYNC"/>
     </logger>
 <root>
  <priority value="debug"/>
```

```
    <appender-ref ref="ASYNC"/>
   </root>
</log4j:configuration>
```

Sample Use of AsyncAppender

The program in Listing 3-12, AsyncLogging.java, uses the async.xml file defined in Listing 3-11 as its configuration source. This example simply sets the buffer size to 4 for the AsyncAppender being used. The AsyncAppender will not print any message so long as the number of logging events is less than the buffer size. Once the number of logging events exceeds the buffer size, the buffer is flushed and all the messages will be printed.

Listing 3-12. *AsyncLogging.java*

```
package com.apress.logging.log4j;

import org.apache.log4j.*;
import org.apache.log4j.xml.DOMConfigurator;
public class AsyncLogging
{

    //private static Logger logger
    Logger.getLogger(AsyncLogging.class.getPackage().getName());
        private AsyncAppender asyncAppender = null;
    private ConsoleAppender consoleAppender = null;

    /** Creates a new instance of AsyncLogging */
    public AsyncLogging()
    {

        try {
            logger.setAdditivity(false);
            asyncAppender =
(AsyncAppender)logger.getRootLogger().getAppender("ASYNC");
            asyncAppender.setBufferSize(4);
        }catch(Exception e) {
            System.out.println("error: "+e.toString());
        }

    }

    /** This method simply logs the messages
     */
    public void doLogging()
    {
        logger.debug("Hello 1");
        logger.debug("Hello 2");
```

```
        logger.debug("Hello 3");
        //logger.debug("Hello 4");
        //logger.debug("Hello 5");
    }

    /** the main method
     */
    public static void main(String args[])
    {
        AsyncLogging demo = new AsyncLogging();
        demo.doLogging();
    }
}
```

Executing this program will not produce any logging messages, as the buffer size for the AsyncAppender is set to 4, and we are logging only three events. If we uncomment the two other logging events, numbered 4 and 5, and we will see these messages printed in the console as follows:

```
2002-10-13 14:05:34,198 DEBUG [main]   - Hello 1
2002-10-13 14:05:34,218 DEBUG [main]   - Hello 2
2002-10-13 14:05:34,218 DEBUG [main]   - Hello 3
2002-10-13 14:05:34,218 DEBUG [main]   - Hello 4
2002-10-13 14:05:34,218 DEBUG [main]   - Hello 5
```

Sending Logging Information to Remote Destinations

So far we have seen Appender objects that can publish and store logging information locally to a console or a file. It is often also important to be able to distribute the logging information, by sending logging information to a database or to a remote machine, for example. Apache log4j provides other Appender objects to do the job, which I will discuss next.

Logging to a Database with JDBCAppender

Storing logging data in a database serves two purposes: First, the data is persisted, and second, the applications residing outside the domain of the application being logged can access and analyze the data.

The log4j API provides the org.apache.log4j.jdbc.JDBCAppender object, which is capable of putting logging information in a specified database. It does simplistic jobs such as opening a database connection by reading JDBC connection parameters passed to it, writing the data to one or more tables following a specified SQL statement, and closing the connection. We can extend the functionality of the JDBCAppender object to meet our needs. At present, JDBCAppender operates in the following manner:

- It has a buffered implementation. The logging events passed to it are stored in a buffer of a predefined size. Once the buffer reaches its maximum size, the buffer is flushed and the data is written to the table, following the specified SQL statement.

- It opens a single connection to the database and maintains the connection until the appender is closed.

- As the SQL operation can be INSERT, UPDATE, or DELETE for a particular record, JDBCAppender cleverly uses the executeUpdate() method of the java.sql.Statement object. This gives the flexibility to execute any type of SQL statement. The decision whether to insert, update, or delete a particular logging record is up to the application developer and is specified by the SQL statement in the configuration file. JDBCAppender will make no decision regarding the nature of the SQL statement. It merely executes the SQL statement passed to it.

- Although JDBCAppender does not decide the nature of the SQL statement to be executed, it is responsible for maintaining the integrity of the event that is being logged. The methods in JDBCAppender are not synchronized to keep its performance intact. This can create a problem of data integrity. Before all the elements of the buffer are written to the database, another logging request might arrive. The buffer will get the new logging event appended to it. Recognizing this new data in the buffer, JDBCAppender will again try to iterate through the buffer to write all the elements in it to the database. This can lead to attempting to write duplicate data in the database, which will surely result in a database error.

- To avoid the problem just mentioned, after an element of the buffer is written to the database, JDBCAppender stores it in a secondary buffer. In the end, it compares the primary buffer with the elements in the secondary buffer, and removes from the primary buffer all the elements that are present in the secondary buffer. This ensures that no duplicate element is retained in the primary buffer.

- JDBCAppender provides a close() method to release any database resource obtained. In theory, the close() method can be called at any time in an application's lifetime. Moreover, when the application terminates by calling the LogManager.shutdown() method, the close() method of every appender active in the system is called. This might result in a loss of data if the close() method is called before a JDBCAppender instance can finish its writing operation. To make sure that data is not lost, the close() method in the JDBCAppender flushes the primary buffer to ensure that the data already in the buffer gets written to the database.

Configuring JDBCAppender

Before we proceed to an example of JDBCAppender in action, it is important to understand how to configure JDBCAppender objects. JDBCAppender has the configurable bean properties listed in Table 3-8.

Table 3-8. *Bean Properties in the JDBCAppender Class*

Bean Property	Method	Description	Default
bufferSize	SetBufferSize(int)	Sets the buffer size	Default size is 1.
driver	setDriver(String)	Sets the driver class to the specified string	If no driver class is specified, defaults to sun.jdbc.odbc. JdbcOdbcDriver.
layout	SetLayout(String)	Sets the layout to be used	Default layout is org.apache.log4j. PatternLayout.
password	SetPassword(String)	Sets the password against the user name specified to obtain a connection to the database	The user must specify a valid password to access the database.
URL	setURL(String)	Sets the JDBC URL	The URL defaults to an arbitrary value. The user must specify a proper JDBC URL.
user	setUser(String)	Sets the user name necessary to obtain a connection to the specified database	The user must specify a valid user name to access the database.

Creating a Table for Storing Logging Information

Listing 3-13 describes the SQL statement to create a table named LOGGING_DATA to store logging information.

Listing 3-13. *SQL Statement for Creating the LOGGING_DATA Table*

```
CREATE TABLE LOGGING_DATA
("USER_ID" VARCHAR2(10) NOT NULL,
"DATE" VARCHAR2(10) NOT NULL,
"LOGGER" VARCHAR2(50) NOT NULL,
"LEVEL" VARCHAR2(10) NOT NULL,
"MESSAGE" VARCHAR2(1000) NOT NULL)
```

Sample Configuration for JDBCAppender

Listing 3-14, jdbc.properties, describes the configuration file we will be using to log messages to a database table.

Listing 3-14. *Sample JDBCAppender Configuration—Properties Style*

```
#configuring the custom logger
log4j.logger.com.apress.logging.log4j=DEBUG,DB

log4j.appender.DB=org.apache.log4j.jdbc.JDBCAppender
log4j.appender.DB.URL=jdbc:odbc:dbdef
log4j.appender.DB.user=system
log4j.appender.DB.password=manager
log4j.appender.DB.sql=INSERT INTO LOGGING_DATA VALUES('%x','%d{yyyy-MM-
dd}','%C','%p','%m')
```

In the configuration file we assign a level of DEBUG and a JDBCAppender to the named logger com.apress.logging.log4j. The JDBCAppender object is given the following configuration parameters:

- Database URL is jdbc:odbc:dbdef, where dbdef is the name of the database we are connecting to.

- The user ID to connect to the database is system and the password is manager.

- The SQL statement to execute is an INSERT statement with the table name LOGGING_DATA and values to be entered into the table. Notice that the values are specified following a PatternLayout (refer to Chapter 2 for details on PatternLayout objects). The values specified follow the same order as the table columns, and the SQL statement inserts the Nested Diagnostic Context (NDC), the date of logging, the fully qualified name of the logger, the level of logging, and finally the logging message itself.

JDBCAppender can also be configured through XML, as Listing 3-15 shows.

Listing 3-15. *Sample JDBCAppender Configuration—XML Style*

```
<?xml version="1.0" encoding="UTF-8" ?>
<!DOCTYPE log4j:configuration SYSTEM "log4j.dtd">
<log4j:configuration>


<appender name="DB" class="org.apache.log4j.jdbc.JDBCAppender">
    <param name="url" value="jdbc:odbc:dbdef"/>
    <param name="user" value="system"/>
    <param name="password" value="manager"/>
  <param name="sql" value="INSERT INTO LOGGING_DATA VALUES
('%x','%d{yyyy-MM-dd}','%C','%p','%m')"/>
</appender>

<logger name="com.apress.logging.log4j" additivity="false">
    <level value="debug"/>
    <appender-ref ref="DB"/>
</logger>
</log4j:configuration>
```

Note that JDBCAppender does not need a layout to be defined explicitly. Instead, the SQL statement passed to it uses a PatternLayout. You will learn more about layouts in the next chapter.

▓**Note** If the application cannot connect to the database when you're using the JDBCAppender example, you will lose any logging information. To handle such situation, use a backup logging destination. For example, you could use FileAppender alongside JDBCAppender. In case the application fails to log to the database, the information can still be logged in a file.

Implementing JMS-Based Logging with JMSAppender

In the previous chapter, we discussed Appender objects that write logging information to the local machine on which an application is running. Most of these Appender objects are synchronous. The previous section mentioned that JDBCAppender has buffered implementation, which means the caller application gets back the control after submitting a logging event to JDBCAppender; it need not wait for the actual writing to the database to finish.

But in the real world, we might want to achieve a complete asynchronous logging activity— that is, the logger application can send a logging message and completely forget about it. A Receiver application can pick up the logging message at a later time and process that message in its own time. This is what message-oriented software is all about. Apache log4j uses this concept of messaging together with the Java Message Service to implement message-oriented logging.

With localized logging concepts such as file-based logging, logging information is scattered across the various locations in which individual application components reside. JMS-based logging becomes very useful for situations in which we want to collect logging information from various distributed components and store it centrally.

What Is JMS?

Because a detailed discussion about JMS is beyond the scope of this book, we will discuss only how log4j fits into the JMS paradigm. JMS allows application developers to create, send, receive, and read messages. The important features of JMS or any messaging API in this sense are as follows:

- *Asynchronous*: The application module issuing messages and the application module receiving messages can operate independently without knowing each other's available interfaces. The Sender and Receiver applications need not be up and running simultaneously.

- *Reliable*: JMS ensures that messages are sent once and only once.

Message-oriented JMS implementations can differ in the way messages are published and consumed, and the time dependency between the Sender and the Receiver. In the next two sections, we will explore the two most popular messaging domains that JMS implements.

Point-to-Point Messaging

Point-to-Point messaging is built around the concepts of Messages, Queues, Senders, and Receivers. It has the following features:

- The Sender sends the Messages to the Queue.

- The Queue retains the Messages until they are consumed.

- Each Message in the Queue has one and only one consumer (the Receiver).

- The Sender and the Receiver have no time dependency. The Receiver can fetch the Message even if it was not running at the time the Message was sent.

- The Receiver or the consumer acknowledges the receipt of the Message.

Publish-Subscribe Messaging

Publish-Subscribe messaging is centered on the concept of Messages, Topic, Publisher, and Subscriber. It has the following features:

- The Sender publishes the Messages to a Topic.

- Each Message can have zero or multiple Subscriber(s).

- The system takes care of distributing Messages to Subscriber(s).

- Publisher(s) and Subscriber(s) have a time dependency. A Subscriber can subscribe to Messages only if it is up and running at the time the Message is published to a Topic.

- Topic(s) retain Messages only as long it takes to distribute them to Subscriber(s) subscribing to the same Topic.

JMS and log4j

Apache log4j provides the org.apache.log4j.net.JMSAppender object to perform JMS-based logging activity. JMSAppender uses the Publish-Subscribe messaging domain to send logging event–related Messages to a specified Topic. Any application interested in a logging event published in a specified Topic will have to subscribe to the same Topic and listen for any Messages arriving to process them.

To connect to a JMS Topic, the JMSAppender object will have to perform these steps:

1. Obtain a connection to the JMS provider.

2. Subscribe to the Topic destination.

3. Create a session to interact with the provider and the Topic.

The JMS provider, rather than the application program, manages the Connection and Topic objects itself. These are called Administered objects. As the various providers manage Connection and other core objects differently, it is best that the providers themselves manage the objects. The application module gains access to these objects through portable interfaces and remains unaffected by the provider's underlying technology.

Whenever the application requires a reference to the Administered objects, it retrieves the JNDIContext object. The retrieval of the JNDIContext object varies from provider to provider. To illustrate this, let's look at two scenarios using the default J2EE (Java 2 Platform, Enterprise Edition) provider and the BEA WebLogic application server.

JNDIContext with J2EE

The J2EE environment provides a default jndi.properties file containing all the information required to retrieve a JNDI context. If you are using the J2EE lightweight application server, use the following command to obtain a JNDI context:

```
InitialContext jndiContext = new InitialContext();
```

Using a no-argument constructor will initialize a context with the default properties specified within the jndi.properties file local to any JMS API being used. For other JMS providers, you need to pass several other configuration parameters to obtain an initial context.

Note For Java Enterprise Edition or J2SDKEE 1.3.1, the `jndi.properties` file is bundled within `j2ee.jar`.

JNDIContext with WebLogic

As we discussed in the previous sections, the underlying technology for `Administered` objects such as `Connection` and `Topic` is different from one vendor to the next. For this reason, to obtain an initial JNDI context from a provider, we need to pass different configuration properties to it. For example, to obtain an initial context from WebLogic, we would use the following:

```
Properties env = new Properties( );
env.put(Context.INITIAL_CONTEXT_FACTORY,"weblogic.jndi.WLInitialContextFactory);
env.put(Context.PROVIDER_URL, "t3://localhost:7001");
InitialContext jndiContext = new InitialContext(env);
```

Other JMS providers, such as JBoss, will require different configuration parameters passed to them.

Configuring JMSAppender

`JMSAppender` collects information about all the required parameters to obtain a JMS connection through configurable bean properties, which are shown in Table 3-9.

Table 3-9. *Configurable Bean Properties in JMSAppender*

Bean Property	Method	Description	Default
initialContext➡FactoryName	setInitialContext➡FactoryName(String)	Sets the initial context factory name	None
locationInfo	SetLocationInfo(Boolean)	If true, the caller's location information is included	false
password	setPassword(String)	Sets the password for using a JMS connection	None
providerURL	setProviderURL(String)	Specifies the URL for the provider (varies from provider to provider)	None
securityCredentials	setSecurity➡Credentials(String)	Sets the security credential attribute required by a few JMS providers	None
securityPrincipalName	setSecurityPrincipal➡Name(String)	Sets the security principal name for the particular provider	None
topicBindingName	setTopicBinding➡Name(String)	Sets the name of the Topic to connect to	None

Continued

Table 3-9. *Continued*

Bean Property	Method	Description	Default
topicConnection FactoryBindingName	setTopicConnection FactoryBindingName(String)	Sets the name of the connection factory object necessary to obtain the Topic connection	None
URLPkgPrefixes	setURLPkgPrefixes(String)	Sets the package prefix property	None
username	setUserName(String)	Sets the user name for obtaining a connection to the provider	None

Not all the configuration parameters are required for every JMS provider we might use. The JMSAppender works with a large number of JMS providers.

▉**Note** For a sample configuration and use of JMSAppender, please refer to the "Distributed Logging Examples" section later in this chapter.

Working with SocketAppender

Any situation in which we want to transfer logging information from one machine to another represents a distributed logging scenario. You have already seen that JMSAppender is very useful for passing logging information from distributed application components to a central location. It is also possible to pass logging information from one location to another using TCP/IP-based raw socket connections.

It may be tricky to choose between using JMS- or socket-based mechanisms to transfer logging information from one machine to another. Although the underlying implementation of any distributed architecture is TCP/IP-based, the difference is in how the JMS and socket communications operate. The choice between JMS-based and raw socket-based communication to transfer logging information depends on the architecture of the application itself. The following few points may help you when you are faced with deciding which logging method to use:

- Employ JMS-based logging when the application follows a distributed architecture. Remember, an application supporting client-server technology is not necessarily distributed. True distributed architecture will have server-side components that the client uses distributed across different locations. In such scenarios, JMS-based logging is the more effective method.

- In a true distributed application scenario, you will always have an application server running. Java-based application servers will often come with JMS support. If your application is using any application server, consider using JMS-based logging.

- Socket-based logging is suitable for normal client-server situations in which many clients are talking to the same server component. If as a part of an application you have to write the server component, it would probably be easier for you to use socket-based logging. Remember, going for a JMS-based solution when you are not using distributed computing will require the extra cost of deploying a JMS provider.

- In any application scenario in which you want to implement an asynchronous logging mechanism, a JMS-based solution would be ideal and easy to implement. If you do not need an asynchronous mechanism, then a socket-based logging mechanism may win over JMS.

`org.apache.log4j.net.SocketAppender` provides a means for transferring logging information to a remote server over TCP/IP. It basically sends the serialized `LoggingEvent` object over the TCP/IP to a remote log server. The `SocketAppender` object has the following features associated with it:

- The remote logging is *nonintrusive*. The timestamp, the `NDC` information, and the location information are preserved according to the client where the logging request was generated.

- The `SocketAppender` object does not use any `Layout` object to format its data. It transmits the `LoggingEvent` object to the server side in a serialized form.

- Logging events are automatically buffered by the native TCP implementation.

Fault Tolerance

The `SocketAppender` implementation is fault tolerant. It can handle or tries to resolve different network-related problems such as a link being down or link speed being slow. Typically, `SocketAppender` attempts to do the following in case there is a fault:

- If the server is reachable, log events will eventually arrive at the server.

- If the remote server is down and not reachable, logging events are dropped. But as soon as the server comes back, logging activity starts transparently. This transparent connection is accomplished by a connector thread, which attempts to connect to the remote server periodically.

- If the connection to the server is slow but faster than the rate of logging event production, the client will benefit from the native TCP/IP buffered implementation, and it will not be affected by the link speed.

- If the link speed is slower than the rate of logging-event production, the client will suffer because it can only go with the network speed.

- If the network link is up but the server is down, the client will not be blocked, but log events will be lost due to server unavailability.

- If the network link is down but the server is alive, the client will be blocked until it times out (normal TCP/IP timeout) or the network link comes back to life.

- `SocketAppender` does not get garbage collected automatically. It is important that the application code calls the `close()` method of `SocketAppender` or the `shutdown()` method of `LogManager` before exiting the application to make sure that `SocketAppender` is closed. However, if the JVM (Java virtual machine) exits before `SocketAppender` can close gracefully, untransmitted data in the pipe might be lost.

Configuring SocketAppender

`SocketAppender` has the configurable bean properties listed in Table 3-10. Notice from the list of configurable bean properties that you can configure `SocketAppender` to retry to connect the destination server by setting the `reconnectionDelay` property. This is a unique feature and helps achieving a fault tolerant logging system.

Table 3-10. *Configurable Bean Properties in SocketAppender*

Bean Property	Method	Description	Default
locationInfo	setLocationInfo(boolean)	Sets the location information parameter to true or false	false
port	setPort(int)	Sets the port number to connect to	4,560
reconnectionDelay	setReconnectionDelay(int)	Number of milliseconds after which the connector thread should try to reconnect to the server	30,000 milliseconds
remoteHost	setRemoteHost(String)	Sets the remote host name	None

▓**Tip** For a sample configuration file and detailed use of SocketAppender, please refer to the "Distributed Logging Examples" section later in this chapter.

Logging to Windows NT Event Log with NTEventLogAppender

For programs that perform system-level operations, we might need to send log information to the event log of a particular OS. In Java, we might interact with an OS by using Java Native Interface (JNI). org.apache.log4j.net.NTEventLogAppender offers the flexibility to do this.

Because the log4j API is written in Java, to access the Windows NT event log, it uses JNI to talk to an NTEventLogAppender.dll file. This file interacts with the Windows NT event log and writes the logging information there.

▓**Caution** Please do not forget to place the NTEventLogAppender.dll file in a location in the system path. Otherwise, you will see a java.lang.UnsatisfiedLinkError.

The NTEventLogAppender object is very simple to use and has the configurable bean properties shown in Table 3-11.

Table 3-11. *Configurable Bean Properties in NTEventLogAppender*

Bean Property	Method	Description	Default
layout	SetLayout(String)	Sets the layout to be used with this appender	TTCCLayout
source	setSource(String)	Sets the source name for this event log	log4j

Listing 3-16 presents a sample NTEventLogAppender configuration.

Listing 3-16. *Sample NTEventLogAppender Configuration—Properties Style*

```
#configuring the custom logger
log4j.logger.com.apress.logging.log4j=DEBUG,NT

#configuring the NT appender
log4j.appender.NT=org.apache.log4j.nt.NTEventLogAppender
log4j.appender.NT.layout=org.apache.log4j.SimpleLayout
```

This example configuration file provides a SimpleLayout object to NTEventLogAppender. Simply execute the example program with this configuration file. Once finished, if we open the Event Viewer of a Windows NT/Windows 2000/Window XP system, we will see the events logged against the source name Log4j in the application log section. In each event we will find the logging information being stored.

E-mail the Logging Message—SMTPAppender

The greatest feature of a logging API like log4j is that it does not restrict logging activity to mere debug traces. Moreover, as we have seen from the discussions of several Appender objects, these objects constitute a powerful feature for distributing logging information to various components such as databases, NT event logs, sockets, etc. You can exploit this useful feature to achieve data-distribution capability without having to write a separate application module.

One example of this great feature is SMTPAppender. Imagine you are writing an order-processing application that confirms a customer's order as soon as it is received. One traditional solution to this problem is to collect the order information and pass it to a separate mailing application to e-mail it to the user. With the help of SMTPAppender, we can do this without writing even a single line of extra code.

org.apache.log4j.net.SMTPAppender is a powerful Appender object capable of sending logging information using the Simple Mail Transfer Protocol (SMTP). Table 3-12 shows the SMTPAppender object's configurable bean properties.

Table 3-12. *Configurable Bean Properties in SocketAppender*

Bean Property	Method	Description	Default
BufferSize	setBufferSize(int)	Sets the size of the cyclic buffer storing the logging event	512 events
evaluatorClass	setEvaluatorClass(String)	Sets the name of the evaluator class to use to check for any triggering condition.	DefaultEvaluator
from	setFrom(String)	Sets the sender's e-mail address	None

Continued

Table 3-12. *Continued*

Bean Property	Method	Description	Default
layout	setLayout(String)	Sets the layout to format the logging information	None
locationInfo	setLocationInfo(boolean)	Specifies whether the location information should be included in the logging information	false
SMTPHost	setSMTPHost(String)	Sets the name of the SMTP host to be used to send e-mails	None
subject	setSubject(String)	Sets the e-mail's subject	None
to	SetTo(String)	Sets the recipient's e-mail address	None

The evaluatorClass property mentioned in Table 3-12 is worth discussing. SMTPAppender can have an evaluator class attached to it. This evaluator class can evaluate each logging event and decide on a triggering condition to tell the SMTPAppender to fire the e-mail activity. The triggering condition can be anything application-specific, such as a logging event that has a message with an ERROR level. The default evaluator class that SMTPAppender uses is an inner class named DefaultEvaluator. The DefaultEvaluator class checks only whether the level associated with the logging event is greater than or equal to the ERROR level's value.

If the triggering condition is not met, the event is stored in a cyclic buffer with a default size of 512 events. As soon as a logging event arrives that satisfies the triggering condition, all the events from the buffer are retrieved and e-mailed to the recipient.

Listing 3-17 presents a sample configuration for SMTPAppender using smtp.mail.yahoo.com as the SMTP server. You can replace this with any other SMTP server you are using. The to attribute defines the recipient's e-mail address, and from defines the sender's e-mail address. The subject attribute defines the subject of the e-mail, and finally we assign an org.apache.log4j.SimpleLayout object to format the logging information to appear within the body of the e-mail.

Listing 3-17. *Sample SMTPAppender Configuration—Properties Style*

```
#configuring the custom logger
log4j.logger.com.apress.logging.log4j=DEBUG,SMTP

#configuring the SMTP appender
log4j.appender.SMTP=org.apache.log4j.net.SMTPAppender
log4j.appender.SMTP.SMTPHost=smtp.mail.yahoo.com
log4j.appender.SMTP.to=clientname@mailserver.com
log4j.appender.SMTP.subject=Testing the appender
log4j.appender.SMTP.from=yourname@mailserver.com
log4j.appender.SMTP.layout=org.apache.log4j.SimpleLayout
```

With this configuration file, execute the sample program. Remember, SMTPAppender relies on the JavaMail API (mail.jar) and Java Activation API (activation.jar). Make sure that these two .jar files are in your classpath along with the log4j-specific .jar file.

Once executed, we will see the messages are going to the client e-mail address. In our example program, a message with a level of ERROR meets the triggering condition, and thus SMTPAppender sends the e-mail with all the logging events to the specified client e-mail address.

Logging Through Telnet—TelnetAppender

On certain occasions we might want to give remote users access to the logging information we produce from an application. This is particularly important when we want to manage an application remotely. In this case, we are publishing logging data locally and want to give read-only access to the remote user. The best way of doing this is to use the existing Telnet protocol. Remote users can log in to the local machine using Telnet protocol and can read the logging information we want them to see.

The log4j API provides org.apache.log4j.net.TelnetAppender for us to enable this feature. TelnetAppender writes the data to a read-only socket. TelnetAppender is a multithreaded program that opens a server socket connection to a port and listens for any connection made to the same port. As soon as a connection signal arrives, it adds the connection source information to a buffer. Next, whenever a logging request arrives to the TelnetAppender, it writes the data to all the active connection sockets.

The TelnetAppender object uses the default Telnet port 23. Optionally, any other port can be specified. The maximum number of connections it can handle simultaneously is 20. TelnetAppender requires a specific layout to format logging data.

TelnetAppender is ideal when used in conjunction with a servlet. A servlet handles multiple client connections at one point in time. Also, using TelnetAppender for server logging activity allows multiple remote managers to obtain logging information in real time. This is great when remote management of an application is critical.

TelnetAppender—An Exercise

I encourage you to implement TelnetAppender with a servlet as an exercise. Remember, there is not much magic to TelnetAppender. You need only to configure your Logger object to use the TelnetAppender.

Distributed Logging Examples

JMSAppender and SocketAppender are two classic examples of distributing the log messages. In JMSAppender, any interested party can subscribe to the logging messages that are published to a JMS queue. On the other hand, SocketAppender transfers the logging information to a predefined remote host through a particular port. Next, we will see some example programs illustrating the use of JMSAppender and SocketAppender.

The Scenario

Let us consider a section of a hypothetical banking application. The Account Manager application provides two methods for depositing and withdrawing money from individual accounts. The deposit() and withdraw() methods perform the operations to deposit and withdraw money to and from an account. The amount deposited is added to the balance. The `withdraw()` method allows withdrawal only if there are sufficient funds available, and then deducts the amount withdrawn from the current balance. If the balance is not enough, the Account Manager application will notify the user.

The application logs activities for both of these methods and uses the user name as the `NDC` information. The application also logs both the success and failure of each operation. Listing 3-18, `AdvancedLogging.java`, is a sample implementation of the described business process of the Account Manager application.

Listing 3-18. *AdvancedLogging.java*

```java
package com.apress.logging.log4j;

import org.apache.log4j.Logger;
import org.apache.log4j.NDC;
public class AdvancedLogging
{
    private static Logger logger =
Logger.getLogger(AdvancedLogging.class.getPackage().getName());
    private  String userName = null;
    private double balance;

    /** Creates a new instance of AdvancedLogging */
    public AdvancedLogging(String user)
    {
        this.userName = user;
    }
    /**
     *Deposit some amount
     */
    public void deposit(double amount)
    {
        NDC.push(userName);
        balance += amount;
        logger.info("Deposited "+amount+" new balance: "+balance);
        NDC.pop();
    }
    /**
     *withdraw some amount
     */
    public void withdraw(double amount)
    {
        NDC.push(userName);
        if(balance>=amount)
        {
            balance -= amount;
            logger.info("Withdrawn "+amount+" new balance: "+balance);
        }else
        {
```

```
        logger.error("Failed to withdraw: balance: "+balance+" attempted
withdraw: "+amount);
        }
        NDC.pop();
    }
}

    public static void main(String args[])
    {
        AdvancedLogging demo = new AdvancedLogging("sam");
        demo.depositBalance(100.50);
        demo.withDraw(80);
        demo.withDraw(50);
    }
}
```

A JMSAppender Example

Listing 3-19, jms.properties, shows the sample configuration file we will use to configure
JMSAppender.

Listing 3-19. *jms.properties*

```
#configuring the custom logger
log4j.logger.com.apress.logging.log4j=DEBUG,JMS

#configuring the JMS appender
log4j.appender.JMS=org.apache.log4j.net.JMSAppender
log4j.appender.JMS.topicConnectionFactoryBindingName=TopicConnectionFactory
log4j.appender.JMS.topicBindingName=loggingTopic
```

In this example, we use the JMS provider implemented by the J2EE 1.3.1. To work with J2EE,
the JMSAppender object will simply need to create a default JNDIContext object by using the following line of code:

```
InitialContext jndiContext = new InitialContext();
```

The only configuration items that we pass to JMSAppender are topicConnectionFactoryBindingName
and topicBindingName. Notice the Topic name we are using is loggingTopic.

With this minimum configuration, we will be able to use JMSAppender in our sample application. We also need a Subscriber application that will read the messages posted in loggingTopic.
We will create a JMS sample program that listens to loggingTopic and prints the relevant information to the console. It performs the following steps to subscribe to the named JMS Topic and
then read the message sent to it:

1. The program obtains an initial JNDI context.

2. It creates a connection factory object with the name TopicConnectionFactory.

3. The program then uses the Topic name passed through the command line at program
   startup and creates a Topic object.

4. It obtains a connection to the `Topic` and opens a session with the `AUTO_ACKNOWLEDGE` mode. This means that the `Subscriber` will automatically acknowledge the receipt of the message. As soon as this receipt is sent, the `Topic` will no longer retain the message.

5. The program subscribes to the `Topic`.

6. A custom message listener object, `LogMessageListener`, is attached to the `Subscriber` object created with the `Topic` session.

7. The `Subscriber` is now ready to listen to the `Topic` for any messages.

Listing 3-20, `JMSLogSubscriber.java`, is a sample implementation of a JMS `Subscriber`.

Listing 3-20. *JMSLogSubscriber.java*

```
package com.apress.logging.log4j;

import javax.jms.*;
import javax.naming.*;

public class JMSLogSubscriber {

    /** Creates a new instance of JMSLogSubscriber */
    public JMSLogSubscriber() {
    }

    public static void main(String args[]) {
        Context ctx;
        Topic topic;
        TopicSubscriber topicSubscriber;
        TextMessage message;
        TopicConnectionFactory topicFactory;
        TopicConnection topicConnection;
        TopicSession topicSession;
        //collect the topic name from command line
        String topicName = args[0];
        try {
            //creating a default J2EE initial context
            ctx = new InitialContext();
            //obtaining the topic connection factory
            topicFactory =
(TopicConnectionFactory)ctx.lookup("TopicConnectionFactory");
            //creating the topic
            topic = (Topic)ctx.lookup(topicName);
            //opening a topic connection
            topicConnection = topicFactory.createTopicConnection();
            //creating a session to AUTO_ACKNOWLEDGE the receipt of the
            //message
            topicSession = topicConnection.createTopicSession(false,
```

```
Session.AUTO_ACKNOWLEDGE);
            //subscribe to the topic
            topicSubscriber = topicSession.createSubscriber(topic);
            //custom listener to listen to the topic for any message and
            //handle it
            LogMessageListener listener = new LogMessageListener();
            //adding the listener to this subscriber
            topicSubscriber.setMessageListener(listener);
            //start the session
            topicConnection.start();
        }catch(Exception e) {
            //could use log4j here as well.
            e.printStackTrace();
        }
    }
}
```

This program uses a custom listener object to listen to the Topic for any message. There is an alternative to this technique. The Subscriber can call the receive() method to obtain any message from the Topic. However, this is a synchronous mode of receiving and processing messages. The receive() method explicitly fetches the messages from the Topic. This method can block until a message arrives or can timeout if a message does not arrive within a specified time limit. By attaching a MessageListener object to the Subscriber, the Subscriber can receive the message asynchronously. As soon as a message arrives, the JMS provider will notify the MessageListener by invoking its onMessage() method.

Listing 3-21, LogMessageListener.java, is a MessageListener implementation for listening to a Topic. It provides an implementation for the onMessage() method. Within the onMessage() method, it checks for the message type. JMSAppender posts LoggingEvent objects as the ObjectMessage type to the Topic. Thus, LogMessageListener checks for the ObjectMessage, casts it back to the LoggingEvent object, and obtains all the information from the LoggingEvent object.

Listing 3-21. *LogMessageListener.java*

```java
package com.apress.logging.log4j;

import javax.jms.*;
import org.apache.log4j.spi.LoggingEvent;

public class LogMessageListener implements MessageListener{

    /** Creates a new instance of LogMessageListener */
    public LogMessageListener() {
    }

    /**
    *This method listens to any message coming to the subscribe topic,
     checks if correct type
    *and prints the content.
    ***/
```

```
public void onMessage(Message message) {
    TextMessage msg = null;
    try {
       if(message instanceof ObjectMessage){
           ObjectMessage obj =  (ObjectMessage)message;
            LoggingEvent event = (LoggingEvent)obj.getObject();
            }
    } catch (JMSException e) {
        //log exception
        e.printStackTrace();
    } catch (Throwable t) {
        //log exception
        e.printStackTrace();
    }
  }
}
```

The LogMessageListener prints only the logger name and the message encapsulated within the LoggingEvent object. Arguably, it can extract all the information from the LoggingEvent object and process it in the way it wants to. This simple example demonstrates how JMS works with log4j.

Executing the JMS-Based Logging Example

To see the example in action, we need to go through the steps presented in the next sections.

Starting the J2EE JMS Provider

First, make sure that j2ee.jar is included in the classpath. Now start up the J2EE application server with the following command:

```
j2ee -verbose
```

▓**Tip** Remember to set the J2EE_HOME environment to point to the j2ee location.

Creating the Topic

Next, create a new Topic named loggingTopic and add it to the JMS destination with the following command:

```
j2eeadmin -addJmsDestination loggingTopic topic
```

Running the Subscriber

Once the Topic is added to the JMS destination, start JMSLogSubscriber with the following command:

```
java -Djms.properties=%J2EE_HOME%config/jms_client.properties
com.apress.logging.log4j.JMSLogSubscriber loggingTopic
```

Notice that we pass the Topic name loggingTopic as a command-line parameter to the program. Also, we provide the JMS configuration parameters to the J2EE runtime via the jms_client. properties file, which is bundled with J2EE.

Running the Client

Now we are ready to execute our sample program. We will pass the jms.properties file as the log4j configuration file to the runtime. Also, we will provide the JMS configuration parameters to the J2EE runtime via the jms_client.properties file, which is bundled with J2EE.

```
java -Dlog4j.configuration=jms.properties -
Djms.properties=%J2EE_HOME%config/jms_client.properties
com.apress.logging.log4j.AdvancedLogging
```

Executing this program will post all the logging information to the Topic named loggingTopic. In the Subscriber console, we will see the following messages arriving:

```
Message received...
Message received:
The logger name: com.apress.logging.log4j
The message: Deposited 100.5 new balance: 100.5
Message received...
Message received:
The logger name: com.apress.logging.log4j
The message: Withdrawn 80.0 new balance: 20.5
Message received...
Message received:
The logger name: com.apress.logging.log4j
The message: Failed to withdraw: balance: 20.5 attempted withdraw: 50.0
```

Note that all the logging messages are printed in the console, and the application does not terminate even after the logging message is passed to the Topic. This is because the Topic connection is closed only within the close() method of the JMSAppender. If we explicitly call the close() method of the JMSAppender or call the LogManager.shutdown() method as soon as we finish, the Topic connection will be closed and the console will be released.

▓**Note** JMS-based logging ensures the delivery of logging information to the Receiver but does not guarantee time. The logging information passed to the Receiver may not be chronological. One way to get around this problem is to use NDC information for each logging request with the timestamp from each sender. However, it is up to you to decide the best way to deal with this problem for your particular situation.

A SocketAppender Example

Writing logging event data to a remote server is easy—SocketAppender will do the job for us. We just need to pass to it the host name, the port, etc., as a part of the configurable bean properties. We also need a server program that can accept the socket connection opened by SocketAppender and process the incoming data. Listing 3-22, LoggingServer.java, is an example of a server-side program that accepts the data sent to it. It listens to an arbitrary port, 1000. After it receives data from the socket connection, it converts the data to the agreed LoggingEvent object and extracts all the data from it.

Listing 3-22. *LoggingServer.java*

```java
package com.apress.logging.log4j;

import java.net.ServerSocket;
import java.net.Socket;
import java.io.ObjectInputStream;
import java.io.BufferedInputStream;

import org.apache.log4j.spi.LoggingEvent;

public class SocketServer implements Runnable{

    private String portNumber = null;
    private ServerSocket serverSocket = null;
    private Socket socket = null;
    private ObjectInputStream inStream = null;
    private LoggingEvent event = null;
    /** Creates a new instance of SocketServer */
    public SocketServer(String portNumber) {
        this.portNumber = portNumber;
        try {
            //listen to the port specified
            serverSocket = new ServerSocket(Integer.parseInt(portNumber));
            socket = serverSocket.accept();
            //creating a ObjectInputStream from the socket input stream
            inStream = new ObjectInputStream(new
BufferedInputStream(socket.getInputStream()));
            new Thread(this).start();
        }catch(Exception e) {
            //log exception
            e.printStackTrace();
        }
    }


    public void run() {
        try {

            while(true) {

                //cast back to the LoggingEvent object
                event = (LoggingEvent)inStream.readObject();
                //print the mesage and logger name in this logging event
            }
```

```
    }catch(Exception e) {
        //log exception
        e.printStackTrace();
    }
}

public static void main(String args[]) {
    String port = args[0];
    new SocketServer(port);
}
}
```

Notice that SocketServer is a thread-based program, and in the run() method it is constantly listening to the port for any incoming messages. As soon as a message arrives, it is capable of printing the message's content.

Listing 3-23, socket.properties, shows the configuration file required to send the logging information from the example program in Listing 3-18.

Listing 3-23. *socket.properties*

```
#configuring the custom logger
log4j.logger.com.apress.logging.log4j=DEBUG,SOCKET

#configuring the SOCKET appender
log4j.appender.SOCKET=org.apache.log4j.net.SocketAppender
log4j.appender.SOCKET.remoteHost=oemcomputer
log4j.appender.SOCKET.port=1000
```

Running the SocketAppender Sample Program

To see SocketAppender in action, we will need to run the SocketServer program and have it listen to the same port as specified in socket.properties (i.e., 1000). Make sure that SocketServer and SocketAppender both talk to the same port. The host in this example is a machine named oemcomputer where the ServerSocket program is running.

Start up the server program with the following command:

```
java com.apress.logging.log4j.SocketServer 1000
```

Now try the client program by passing it socket.properties as the configuration file.

```
java -Dlog4j.configuration=socket.properties
com.apress.logging.log4j.AdvancvedLogging
```

The following messages will arrive in the server-side console:

```
THE LOGGER NAME: com.apress.logging.log4j
THE MESSAGE: Deposited 100.5 new balance: 100.5
THE LOGGER NAME: com.apress.logging.log4j
THE MESSAGE: Withdrawn 80.0 new balance: 20.5
THE LOGGER NAME: com.apress.logging.log4j
THE MESSAGE: Failed to withdraw: balance: 20.5 attempted withdraw: 50.0
```

Sending Log Messages to a Database

Executing this program with the `jdbc.properties` file in Listing 3-14 will write the data to the database. Figure 3-2 presents an HTML report of the data stored in the table `LOGGING_DATA`.

Figure 3-2. *The LOGGING_DATA table*

Perhaps you have noticed that you don't have to do any JDBC programming to write the data to the database. It is all done within `JDBCAppender`. Also, notice this example demonstrates the power of log4j; the destination of the logging information can be changed by merely changing the configuration file passed to it, requiring no code change at all.

Final Words

In this chapter, we have discussed several `Appender` objects that log4j offers. Table 3-13 presents a brief summary of all the appenders we have covered.

Table 3-13. *Usage of Various Appenders*

Appender	Functionality	Usage
ConsoleAppender	Writes the log messages to the console.	Very basic logging mechanism. By default, the information in the console is volatile and is not stored unless piped to another destination, such as a file.
FileAppender	Writes the log messages to a specified file.	Used when the logging information needs to be persistent.
RollingFileAppender	Writes the log messages to files and rolls the files based on size.	Best used when the log file is to be kept under a certain size for better viewing or processing.
DailyRollingFileAppender	Writes log messages to a file and rolls the file based on date and time.	Best suited for applications with high user activity and daily usage. Logs are rolled each day, which means it is easier to track history.

Appender	Functionality	Usage
JDBCAppender	Logs the messages to a database.	Best used when the structure of logging information is important and used for further data analysis.
JMSAppender	Logs the messages in an asynchronous manner using JMS technology.	Best used when performance is critical and overhead of synchronous logging needs to be optimized.
SocketAppender	Sends the log messages to another machine by opening a socket connection.	Best used to distribute the logging message to a remote logging server.
SMTPAppender	Sends the logging messages to recipients by e-mail.	Best suited for tracking down critical information such as error conditions, or new customer enrollment, and e-mailing them to relevant people.
TelnetAppender	Sends log messages to a read-only socket.	Best suited for remote monitoring of logging data over TCP/IP.

Conclusion

In this chapter, you have examined different Appender objects available in log4j, studied the configurable properties of each Appender, and seen examples of how to configure them through properties files and XML. You have also seen that some of the Appender objects can be configured only through XML-style configuration. You learned that log4j offers logging capabilities for stand-alone and distributed applications, and that logging information can be sent to remote destinations using technologies such as JMS, SMTP, and Telnet.

Although, log4j provides a substantial variety of Appender objects to meet different application scenarios, the coverage may not be enough just for the application you are developing. Maybe you need something special. Don't despair—in Chapter 6, you'll learn how to write your own specialized Appender objects to meet the demands of your application.

■ ■ ■

## CHAPTER 4

Formatting Logging Information in log4j

In the previous chapters, we discussed the core objects in the log4j API, and learned how they interact with each other to produce flexible logging messages. We saw that the initiation of a logging process starts with Logger objects. The encapsulated logging information is passed to Appender objects, and Appender objects use Layout objects to format the logging information in a human-readable way before publishing the logging information to a destination.

How logging information is structured is very important. In a real-life application, logging information constitutes more than just debugging messages—it can contain vital data about software modules, how they are interacting with each other, and other useful information that can be reused to maintain and debug the application modules. Often it may be necessary to post logging information to another error-processing program running on a remote machine. In such scenarios, it becomes important to agree on a structure for the logging information. This is where Layout objects come into the picture.

Apache log4j provides various Layout objects, each of which can format logging data according to various layouts. It is also possible to create a Layout object that formats logging data in an application-specific way. In this chapter, we will examine the Layout objects within log4j and learn how to use them in an application.

The Layout Hierarchy

The structure of logging information can vary in terms of the message content, the type of content, and the way the information is presented. But in abstract terms, all logging information can be organized into a header, a body, and a footer. The header may present an introduction to the message; the body contains the logging information; and the footer section can contain some hint about the content of the message. You can see how this resembles the physical documents that people deal with everyday. Bearing this idea in mind, log4j provides an abstract class called Layout that offers a skeleton implementation of all the common operations. All other individual Layout objects are basically subtypes of this abstract superclass.

Individual Layout objects differ in the styles they use to format the logging information passed to them. These individual Layout objects inherit all the common operations from their abstract superclass and implement their own formatting methods. They may override and provide their own implementation of any method in the base class. Figure 4-1 depicts the class diagram of different Layout objects within the log4j API.

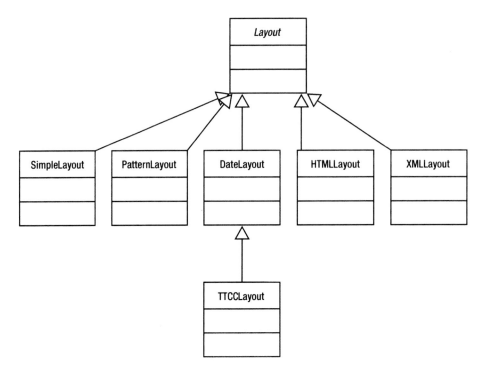

Figure 4-1. *The Layout object hierarchy*

All Layout objects receive a LoggingEvent object from the Appender objects. The Layout objects then retrieve the message argument from the LoggingEvent and apply the appropriate ObjectRenderer to obtain the String representation of the message, as discussed in the previous chapter.

The Layout Objects in log4j

The top-level class in the hierarchy is the abstract class org.apache.log4j.Layout. This is the base class for all other Layout classes in the log4j API. This class provides a skeleton implementation of all the common operations across all other Layout objects and declares two abstract methods, listed in Table 4-1, specifically for the subclasses to override.

Table 4-1. *Abstract Methods in the Layout Class*

Method	Description
public abstract boolean ignoresThrowable()	This method indicates whether the logging information handles any java.lang.Throwable object passed to it as a part of the logging event. If the Layout object handles the Throwable object, then the Layout object does not ignore it, and returns false.
public abstract String format(LoggingEvent event)	Individual layout subclasses will implement this method for layout-specific formatting.

Apart from these `abstract` methods, the `Layout` class provides concrete implementation for the methods listed in Table 4-2.

Table 4-2. *Other Methods in the Layout Class*

Method	Description
`public String getContentType()`	Returns the content type used by the `Layout` objects. The base class returns `text/plain` as the default content type.
`public String getFooter()`	Specifies the footer information of the logging message.
`public String getHeader()`	Specifies the header information of the logging message.

Each subclass can return class-specific information by overriding the concrete implementation of these methods.

As the `Layout` class is defined as `abstract` within an application, we never use this class directly; instead, we work with its subclasses. If none of the default `Layout` objects meet your purpose, then of course you can create your own `XYZLayout` object by extending the `Layout` class. You'll see an example of a custom layout in Chapter 6.

Keeping It Simple—SimpleLayout

`org.apache.log4j.SimpleLayout` provides a very basic structure for the logging message. It includes only the level of the logging information and the logging message itself. As you saw in the previous chapter, the `LoggingEvent` object can contain other information related to the logging activity, such as the time, thread, location information, etc., and producing all this information can clutter the logging output. It can be a painstaking process to cull the necessary information from the large amount of information that a logging event contains. In this case, `SimpleLayout` proves very useful for publishing quick debugging-style messages.

In short, the `SimpleLayout` object performs the following actions:

- It formats the `LoggingEvent` object by including only the level information and the message, and ignores all other information.

- It does not handle the `java.lang.Throwable` instance passed through the logging event, and the `ignoresThrowable()` method returns `true`. This means that no stack trace will be printed as part of the logging message.

An example message formatted with `SimpleLayout` can look like the following:

```
INFO -  "A Message"
```

The formatting structure is the level information, followed by a hyphen sign (-), and the logging message.

Note As `SimpleLayout` is a closed system, there is no configuration parameter for this layout. This object always formats the logging information the same way, with the same style.

Thread-Time-Category-Context—TTCCLayout

TTCCLayout is much more effective in a multiuser environment than the other Layout objects. Before moving on to the other Layout objects available within the log4j API, we will see how log4j handles the multiuser logging environment through TTCCLayout.

The formatting style that the SimpleLayout object adopts is very simplistic. In some cases it might prove useful, and in other cases we may want to publish more detailed information about the logging event. Particularly in multithreaded applications, in which multiple clients are accessing the same application module, it is important to publish the time of logging, the active thread, etc., to distinguish between two separate client activities. One other technique to differentiate between each client is the Nested Diagnostic Context (NDC). All this information can be put into the LoggingEvent object before passing it to the Layout objects.

org.apache.log4j.TTCCLayout does the job of presenting detailed information about a logging event. It extends the org.apache.log4j.helpers.DateLayout class. Typically, it contains the following information as part of the logging message:

- *Thread*: The invoking thread.

- *Time*: The time in terms of number of milliseconds elapsed since the application was started.

- *Category*: The category or the logger used to create this logging event.

- *Context*: The NDC information. This information is not automatically included in the LoggingEvent object; we have to include it deliberately. Thus, this is an optional output from TTCCLayout—and even though the NDC setting is enabled, TTCCLayout might not display any NDC data if the LoggingEvent does not contain any.

▦**Note** The TTCCLayout object ignores any java.lang.Throwable instance passed to the LoggingEvent.

The Mandatory Information

The properties discussed in the previous section are optional and can be configured with TTCCLayout to attach to a logging message. None of those are mandatory properties. For a given TTCCLayout configuration, you may decide to invalidate all those configurable parameters. Then there is not much point in using TTCCLayout. However, should you decide to invalidate those parameters, TTCCLayout will still give out the following information:

- Level: The level of the logging message

- Message: The logging message itself

You will now see how to write a simple program to illustrate the formatting that the TTCCLayout object provides. For the sake of completeness, we will first configure the logger used in this example programmatically. Later we'll configure it through a configuration file.

Configuring TTCCLayout Programmatically

To perform the programmatic configuration, we will obtain an instance of a named Logger and attach a ConsoleAppender to the logger instance. To format the logging message, we will also attach a TTCCLayout object to the ConsoleAppender. In this example, we will instantiate a TTCCLayout object with the yyyy-MM-dd date pattern. This will cause the date to be formatted as "2005-10-20," for example. In the computeSquareRoot() method, we will create one NDC, and the String value of the double argument will be passed to it. After computing the square root, we will print the square root value with the logger.info() method. Take a look at the code presented in Listing 4-1, LayoutDemo.java.

Listing 4-1. *LayoutDemo.java*

```java
package com.apress.logging.log4j;

import org.apache.log4j.Logger;
import org.apache.log4j.ConsoleAppender;
import org.apache.log4j.TTCCLayout;
import org.apache.log4j.NDC;

public class LayoutDemo
{
    private static Logger logger =
Logger.getLogger(LayoutDemo.class.getPackage().getName());
    private ConsoleAppender appender = null;
    private TTCCLayout layout = null;

    /** Creates a new instance of LayoutDemo */
    public LayoutDemo()
    {
        //set the parent additivity to false
        logger.setAdditivity(false);

         //initialize the layout
        layout = new TTCCLayout("yyyy-MM-dd");

        //initialize the console appender with the layout
        appender = new ConsoleAppender(layout,"System.out");

        //adding the console appender to the logger
        logger.addAppender(appender);

    }
```

```
public void computeSquareRoot(double number)
{
    NDC.push(new Double(number).toString());
    double sqrt = Math.sqrt(number);
    logger.info("The sqrt value: "+sqrt);
    NDC.pop();

}

public static void main(String args[])
{
    LayoutDemo demo = new LayoutDemo();
    demo.computeSquareRoot(22);
    demo.computeSquareRoot(44);
}
}
```

■**Note** Notice the use of NDC.push() at the beginning of the computeSquareRoot() method and NDC.pop() at then end of the computeSquareRoot() method.

Executing this program will produce the following output to System.out in a console:

```
2002-10-17 [main] INFO com.apress.logging.log4j 44.0 - The sqrt value:
6.6332495807108
```

The output can be divided into the parts described in Table 4-3.

Table 4-3. *TTCCLayout Formatting Structure*

Information	Meaning
2002-10-17	The date of the logging activity. (Time elapsed from the start of the application can also be displayed.)
[main]	The thread invoking the logging request.
INFO	The logging level.
com.apress.logging.log4j	The name of the logger.
44.00	The NDC value.
-	The separator.
The sqrt value	The logging message.

As is evident from the structure of the logging information, TTCCLayout has seven constituents for the logging information it publishes. The appearance of each constituent in the final logging information depends on whether the information has been supplied as a part of the LoggingEvent object to the TTCCLayout object. The TTCCLayout object controls the appearance of the different parts of the logging messages through the bean properties listed in Table 4-4.

Table 4-4. *Bean Properties in the TTCCLayout Class*

Bean Property	Method	Description	Default
categoryPrefixing	setCategoryPrefixing(boolean)	Specifies whether the name of the category or the logger should be a part of the logging information	true
contextPrinting	setContextPrinting(boolean)	Specifies whether the NDC should be a part of the logging information	true
threadPrinting	setThreadPrinting(boolean)	Specifies whether the thread information should be a part of the logging information	true

As the TTCCLayout class is a direct subclass of DateLayout, it also inherits the bean properties listed in Table 4-5 from the DateLayout class.

Table 4-5. *Bean Properties Inherited from DateLayout*

Bean Property	Method	Description	Default
dateFormat	setDateFormat(String)	Sets the date format to be used in Java SimpleDateFormat style (e.g., yyyy-MM-dd) or one of the strings NULL, RELATIVE, DATE, ABSOLUTE, or ISO8601	RELATIVE
timeZone	setTimeZone(String)	Time zone specified in the java.util.TimeZone.getTimeZone(String) method (e.g., GMT-8:00)	None

Configuring TTCCLayout via Configuration File

The log4j Layout objects can also be configured through configuration files by setting the bean property values. Listing 4-2 demonstrates how to use a configuration file, ttcc.properties, to configure TTCCLayout.

Listing 4-2. *ttcc.properties*

```
#configuring the root logger
log4j.rootLogger=DEBUG,CONSOLE

#configuring the named logger
log4j.logger.com.apress.logging.log4j=DEBUG, CONSOLE

#configuring the appender CONSOLE
log4j.appender.CONSOLE=org.apache.log4j.ConsoleAppender
log4j.appender.CONSOLE.layout=org.apache.log4j.TTCCLayout
```

```
#configuring the layout TTCCLayout
log4j.appender.CONSOLE.layout.ThreadPrinting=false
log4j.appender.CONSOLE.layout.ContextPrinting=false
log4j.appender.CONSOLE.layout.CategoryPrefixing=false
log4j.appender.CONSOLE.layout.DateFormat=RELATIVE
```

■**Note** While executing the program with this configuration file, remember to turn off the configuration code in the constructor of the program. It makes no sense to do the same configuration in two places.

In this configuration, we disable the ThreadPrinting and ContextPrinting bean properties. As mentioned in Table 4-5, the DateFormat bean property defaults to RELATIVE, which means this program will print the time elapsed, in milliseconds, since the program started.

Executing the example program in Listing 4-1 with this configuration file will result in the following logging information displaying in the console:

```
40 INFO 22.0 - The sqrt value: 4.69041575982343
50 INFO 44.0 - The sqrt value: 6.6332495807108
```

Notice the thread and the NDC information are now not displayed as a part of the logging information, as we have disabled the contextPrinting property.

TTCCLayout can also be configured through XML, as in Listing 4-3.

Listing 4-3. *TTCCLayout Configuration in XML*

```
<?xml version="1.0" encoding="UTF-8" ?>
<!DOCTYPE log4j:configuration SYSTEM "log4j.dtd">
<log4j:configuration>

<appender name="dataAccessLogger" class="org.apache.log4j.ConsoleAppender">
    <param name="threshold" value="debug"/>
    <layout class="org.apache.log4j.TTCCLayout">
        <param name="ThreadPrinting" value="false"/>
        <param name="ContextPrinting" value="false"/>
        <param name="CategoryPrefixing" value="false"/>
        <param name="DateFormat" value="NULL"/>
    </layout>

  </appender>

<logger name="com.apress.logging.log4j" additivity="false">
    <level value="debug"/>
    <appender-ref ref="dataAccessLogger"/>
</logger>
</log4j:configuration>
```

▧**Caution** Do not use the same TTCCLayout instance in two different Appender objects. This is not thread-safe.

The Date—DateLayout

As you have seen in the previous section, the TTCCLayout class uses another class, DateLayout, to format its date- and timestamp-related information. DateLayout is an abstract class that extends the org.apache.log4j.Layout class. It is also a convenience class for handling all date-related formatting tasks, and it accepts a LoggingEvent object and a date format to format the timestamp included in the LoggingEvent object.

The DateLayout class has the bean properties listed in Table 4-5 for setting the parameters of date-related formatting tasks.

The date formats used with DateLayout have the properties listed in Table 4-6.

Table 4-6. *Date Formats in the DateLayout Class*

Date Format	Meaning
NULL	No date or time is displayed.
RELATIVE	Displays the time elapsed after the application was started.
DATE	Formats the date with the dd MMM YYYY HH:mm:ss,SSS pattern—for example, 10 Oct 2002 15:30:39,450. The final SSS represents the time elapsed after the application was started.
ABSOLUTE	Formats a date with the HH:mm:ss,SSS pattern—for example, 10:49:33, 459.
ISO8601	Formats a date with the yyyy-MM-dd HH:mm:ss,SSS pattern—for example, 2002-10-20 10:49:33,459.

Any Layout object that we want to format and publish the date and timestamp information related to logging could use the DateLayout class to do the formatting.

HTMLLayout

The goal of a well-designed system is to make users comfortable with how information is presented to them. Therefore, your application might need to produce logging information in a nice HTML-formatted file. org.apache.log4j.HTMLLayout is an object dedicated to formatting logging information in HTML.

The HTMLLayout class extends the abstract org.apache.log4j.Layout class and overrides the format() method from its base class to provide HTML-style formatting. It is a very simple Layout object that has the configurable bean properties listed in Table 4-7.

Table 4-7. *Bean Properties in HTMLLayout*

Bean Property	Method	Description	Default
contentType	setContentType(String)	Sets the content type of the HTML content	text/html
locationInfo	setLocationInfo(String)	Sets the location information for the logging event	false
title	setTitle(String)	Sets the title for the HTML content	Log4j Log Messages

The HTMLLayout object includes the following as a part of the logging information it displays:

- The time elapsed from the start of the application before a particular logging event was generated.

- The name of the thread that invoked the logging request.

- The level associated with this logging request.

- The name of the logger.

- The optional location information for the program file and the line number from which this logging was invoked.

- The logging message.

- The NDC information.

- Any exception that is generated in the application and needs to be logged. (This is due to the object being able to handle a java.lang.Throwable instance.)

To demonstrate the formatting capability of the HTMLLayout object, we will use the same program presented in Listing 4-1, but pass a different configuration file to configure the logger with HTMLLayout. Listing 4-4 describes this configuration file, html.properties.

Listing 4-4. *html.properties*

```
#configuring the custom logger
log4j.logger.com.apress.logging.log4j=DEBUG,FILE

log4j.appender.FILE=org.apache.log4j.FileAppender
log4j.appender.FILE.File=htmlLayout.html

log4j.appender.FILE.layout=org.apache.log4j.HTMLLayout
log4j.appender.FILE.layout.Title=HTML Layout Demo
log4j.appender.FILE.layout.LocationInfo=true
```

In the configuration file, we assign the FileAppender object the filename htmlLayout.html, and the logging information will be written to this file. The file will be created in the path from which you run the application. The FileAppender in turn uses HTMLLayout to format the logging information. The HTMLLayout object has its LocationInfo bean property set to true and its title bean property set to HTML Layout Demo.

Executing the program with this configuration file will create the htmlLayout.html file containing all the logging information. Figure 4-2 shows this HTML file.

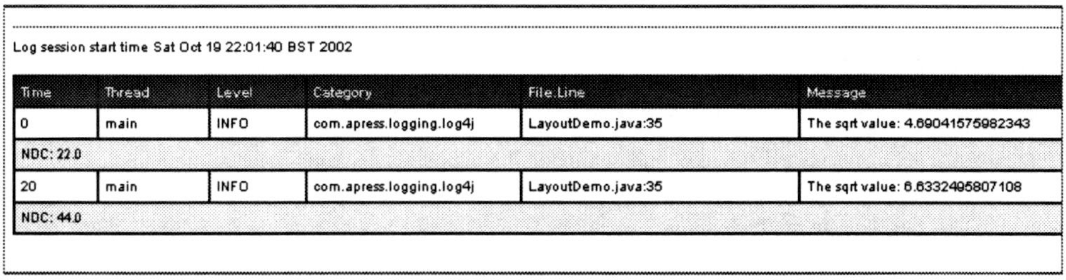

Log session start time Sat Oct 19 22:01:40 BST 2002					
Time	Thread	Level	Category	File:Line	Message
0	main	INFO	com.apress.logging.log4j	LayoutDemo.java:35	The sqrt value: 4.69041575982343
NDC: 22.0					
20	main	INFO	com.apress.logging.log4j	LayoutDemo.java:35	The sqrt value: 6.6332495807108
NDC: 44.0					

Figure 4-2. *The HTML file produced with HTMLLayout*

HTMLLayout can also be configured through XML configuration. Listing 4-5 presents a sample configuration in XML.

Listing 4-5. *HTMLLayout Configuration in XML*

```xml
<?xml version="1.0" encoding="UTF-8" ?>
<!DOCTYPE log4j:configuration SYSTEM "log4j.dtd">
<log4j:configuration>

<appender name="dataAccessLogger" class="org.apache.log4j.ConsoleAppender">
   <param name="threshold" value="debug"/>
     <layout class="org.apache.log4j.TTCCLayout">
       <param name="ThreadPrinting" value="false"/>
       <param name="ContextPrinting" value="false"/>
       <param name="CategoryPrefixing" value="false"/>
       <param name="DateFormat" value="NULL"/>
   </layout>


  </appender>

<appender name="dest" class="org.apache.log4j.FileAppender">
   <param name="file" value="${user.home}/log.html"/>
   <param name="threshold" value="debug"/>
   <param name="immediateFlush" value="true"/>
   <param name="append" value="false"/>


    <layout class="org.apache.log4j.HTMLLayout">
       <param name="Title" value="false"/>
       <param name="LocationInfo" value="true"/>
         </layout>

  </appender>

<appender name="ASYNC" class="org.apache.log4j.AsyncAppender">
         <param name="bufferSize" value="15"/>
           <appender-ref ref="dataAccessLogger"/>
 </appender>
```

```
<logger name="com.apress.logging.log4j" additivity="false">
   <level value="debug"/>
   <appender-ref ref="dest"/>
</logger>
<!--
<root>
  <priority value="debug"/>
  <appender-ref ref="ASYNC"/>
</root>
-->
</log4j:configuration>
```

The Big Advantage

One of the big advantages of having the log file in HTML format is that it can be published as a web page for remote viewing. This provides more flexibility for anybody to look at the logs whenever they need to. Some of the other layouts, such as XML, demand processing of data before it is easily viewed. However, each layout comes with its own advantages and disadvantages.

A Caution About HTMLLayout

Our discussion of HTMLLayout would be incomplete without a quick look at a possible problem with the source file that was generated in the previous example. If you open this file, you will see the HTML code shown in Listing 4-6.

Listing 4-6. *The HTML Source Code Produced by HTMLLayout*

```
<!DOCTYPE HTML PUBLIC "-//W3C//DTD HTML 4.01 Transitional//EN"
"http://www.w3.org/TR/html4/loose.dtd">
<html>
<head>
<title>Log4J Log Messages</title>
<style type="text/css">
<!--
body, table {font-family: arial,sans-serif; font-size: x-small;}
th {background: #336699; color: #FFFFFF; text-align: left;}
-->
</style>
</head>
<body bgcolor="#FFFFFF" topmargin="6" leftmargin="6">
<hr size="1" noshade>
Log session start time Sat Oct 19 22:01:40 BST 2002<br>
<br>
<table cellspacing="0" cellpadding="4" border="1" bordercolor="#224466"
width="100%">
<tr>
<th>Time</th>
<th>Thread</th>
<th>Level</th>
```

```
<th>Category</th>
<th>File:Line</th>
<th>Message</th>
</tr>

<tr>
<td>0</td>
<td title="main thread">main</td>
<td title="Level">INFO</td>
<td title="com.apress.logging.log4j category">com.apress.logging.log4j</td>
<td>LayoutDemo.java:35</td>
<td title="Message">The sqrt value: 4.69041575982343</td>
</tr>
<tr><td bgcolor="#EEEEEE" style="font-size : xx-small;" colspan="6"
title="Nested Diagnostic Context">NDC: 22.0</td></tr>

<tr>
<td>20</td>
<td title="main thread">main</td>
<td title="Level">INFO</td>
<td title="com.apress.logging.log4j category">com.apress.logging.log4j</td>
<td>LayoutDemo.java:35</td>
<td title="Message">The sqrt value: 6.6332495807108</td>
</tr>
<tr><td bgcolor="#EEEEEE" style="font-size : xx-small;" colspan="6"
title="Nested Diagnostic Context">NDC: 44.0</td></tr>
```

Notice that the header information contains the <html> and <body> tags, but the footer for the </html> and </body> tags is completely missing. Clearly, this is not a well-formed HTML file. Some browsers might allow us to use this style of HTML source, but some may not. The question is, why is the footer (i.e., the closing tags) missing?

The answer lies in when the getFooter() method of the HTMLLayout is called. In version 1.2.9 of log4j, the getFooter() method of any Layout object is called when the close() method of the related Appender object is called. This may be a small bug in the API, depending on how the application is performing the logging activity.

Imagine an application module that is a server component handling multiple client calls. For every call, we want to write the logging information to an HTML file. We want the header to be included only once when the HTMLLayout object is initialized. This is done in the setWriter() method of HTMLLayout at initialization. Now the issue is when we want to write the footer. If for every logging request, we want to open a new file and close the file after the logging is over, we can call the getFooter() method after every logging request is formatted. But if we want to include all the logging information in a single file, and that single file contains logging information for more than one logging request, we cannot append the footer information every time.

The best time to call getFooter() is when the Appender objects themselves are no longer needed. For our imaginary application, when we exit our server component (such as the destroy() method in a servlet), we would call the LogManager.shutdown() method to close all the Appender objects. This ensures that the footer is written to the end of the HTML file produced.

In this particular example, in the `computeSquareRoot()` method just before leaving the method, if we call

```
LogManager.shutDown()
```

we would see that the footer information is included in the final HTML file. This may not be ideal, but this is how we have to deal with it in version 1.2.9 of log4j.

XMLLayout

Logging information in HTML format is nice and user-friendly, but is not portable across multiple application modules, and the data is structured nondescriptively. To render logging information in XML format, which is portable, log4j provides the `org.apache.log4j.xml.XMLLayout` object.

The `XMLLayout` object may include the following items from `LoggingEvent` in the final output:

- The logger name
- The timestamp
- The level associated with the logging request
- The invoking thread name
- The logging message
- The `NDC` information
- The `java.lang.Throwable` instance included within the `LoggingEvent`
- The location info for the logging request (turned off by default)

`XMLLayout` follows the document type definition contained in the `log4j.dtd` file to create the XML output. It is important to note that the final output is *not* a well-formed XML file. It may sound surprising, but the purpose of this object is to produce logging information as a series of `<log4j:event>` elements. The final output then can be referenced as an entity to a proper XML file.

■**Note** Please refer to Appendix B for the full `log4j.dtd` listing.

To illustrate this concept, let's reuse the program in Listing 4-1 with the configuration file for `XMLLayout`, `xml.properties`, defined in Listing 4-7.

Listing 4-7. *xml.properties*

```
#configuring the custom logger
log4j.logger.com.apress.logging.log4j=DEBUG,FILE

log4j.appender.FILE=org.apache.log4j.FileAppender
log4j.appender.FILE.File=xmlLayout.xml

log4j.appender.FILE.layout=org.apache.log4j.xml.XMLLayout
log4j.appender.FILE.layout.LocationInfo=true
```

The configuration uses a `FileAppender` along with `XMLLayout` to format the logging information.

Executing the program with this configuration file will write the formatted logging information to the `xmlLayout.xml` file. The content of the file looks similar to the following:

```
<log4j:event logger="com.apress.logging.log4j" timestamp="1035061552691"
level="INFO" thread="main">
<log4j:message><![CDATA[The sqrt value: 4.69041575982343]]></log4j:message>
<log4j:NDC><![CDATA[22.0]]></log4j:NDC>
<log4j:locationInfo class="com.apress.logging.log4j.LayoutDemo"
method="computeSquareRoot" file="LayoutDemo.java" line="35"/>
</log4j:event>

<log4j:event logger="com.apress.logging.log4j" timestamp="1035061552711"
level="INFO" thread="main">
<log4j:message><![CDATA[The sqrt value: 6.6332495807108]]></log4j:message>
<log4j:NDC><![CDATA[44.0]]></log4j:NDC>
<log4j:locationInfo class="com.apress.logging.log4j.LayoutDemo"
method="computeSquareRoot" file="LayoutDemo.java" line="35"/>
</log4j:event>
```

As is evident, the XML output is a series of `<log4j:event>` elements containing child elements to present the logging information. The following code snippet shows how to include this information in a well-formed XML file.

```
<?xml version="1.0" ?>

<!DOCTYPE log4j:eventSet SYSTEM "log4j.dtd" [<!ENTITY logEntity SYSTEM
"xmlLayout.xml">]>

<log4j:eventSet version="1.2" xmlns:log4j="http://jakarta.apache.org/log4j/">
  &logEntity;
</log4j:eventSet>
```

At first sight, this might seem confusing. But the rationale behind it is that it makes the `Layout` object rendering the logging message into XML format and the `Appender` object using this `Layout` independent of each other.

To further illustrate, let's say that you are writing a custom appender. You want the appender to include your company information header with every logging output. You also want the logging information to be published in XML format. In such scenarios, you will override the `doAppend()` method in your custom appender to write the logging information into an XML file. Also, you can include a standard header containing your company information and can still use the existing `XMLLayout` object to format the logging information in its own style. You can then include a reference to the file that the `XMLLayout` object produced as an external `ENTITY` within your XML file containing your company information. Clearly, you have achieved the flexibility of including the XML logging information from the `XMLLayout` object as an `ELEMENT` of another XML content.

▨**Note** XMLLayout can also be configured through an XML configuration file. Because it is just like any other layout configuration in XML style, I am not including an example here. You can find an example in Listing 3-4 in Chapter 3.

Give It a Pattern—PatternLayout

Formatting any piece of information means giving it a pattern that an external entity can recognize and understand. Providing a pattern to the logging information makes it recognizable to a human or a program. Furthermore, if the module producing the logging information and a module receiving the information agree on a pattern beforehand, that information can be processed. This is where PatternLayout becomes useful.

org.apache.log4j.PatternLayout extends the base abstract-class Layout and overrides the format() method to structure logging information according to a supplied pattern. We can supply the pattern either through a configuration file or programmatically. The PatternLayout object has the bean property shown in Table 4-8.

Table 4-8. *Bean Property in PatternLayout*

Bean Property	Method	Description	Default
conversionPattern	setConversionPattern()	Sets the conversion pattern	%r [%t] %p %c ➥ %x - %m%n

PatternLayout can include all the information within the LoggingEvent object in the final message. PatternLayout formats the logging information against a given pattern. The pattern supplied essentially dictates the following items:

- The formatting information is dictated by *format modifiers.*

- The information to be displayed is dictated by *conversion characters.*

Table 4-9 displays all the conversion characters that can be used with PatternLayout. Notice that the PatternLayout does not handle any java.lang.Throwable instance at all.

Table 4-9. *The Conversion Characters for PatternLayout*

Conversion Character	Meaning
c	The Logger used to invoke this logging request. This can take a precision specifier. For instance, in our example, the logger name is com.apress.logging.log4. With a precision specifier c{2}, the logger will be printed as logging.log4j. Notice that only the corresponding numbers of elements from the right-hand side of the full logger name are included in the final output.
C	The fully qualified name of the Logger invoking this logging request. This can also accept a precision specifier as described with conversion character c. Generating the fully qualified name of the logger can be very slow.
d	The date of the logging request. This can also take an optional date specifier. For example, %d{yyyy-MM-dd} will print the date in year-month-day format. If no date format is specified, this uses the ISO8601 format defined within log4j. The performance of java.text.SimpleDateFormat is quite poor; for better results use the DateFormat objects provided with the log4j API.

Conversion Character	Meaning
F	The name of the file from which the logging request was issued.
l	The location information. This information can be quite useful when an application produces any exception stack trace. However, generating this information with log4j can be quite slow. A trade-off has to be made before this feature is used.
L	The line number in the program file from which the logging request was issued.
m	The logging message.
M	The method in the program from which the logging request was issued.
n	Platform-dependent line separator.
p	The level associated with the logging request.
r	The RELATIVE date format displaying the number of milliseconds elapsed from the start of the application before this logging request was issued.
t	The invoking thread.
x	The NDC information.
X	The Message Diagnostic Context (MDC) information. The X conversion character is followed by the key for the MDC. For example, X{clientIP} will print the information stored in the MDC against the key clientIP.
%	The literal percent sign. %% will print a % sign.

The format modifiers used along with PatternLayout are described in Table 4-10.

Table 4-10. *Format Modifiers Used in PatternLayout*

Modifier	Left-Justified	Minimum Length	Maximum Length	Meaning
%10c	No	10 characters	None	Displays the logger name. If the name is less than 10 characters long, then padding is applied to the left side.
%-10c	Yes	10 characters	None	Displays the logger name. If the name is less than 10 characters long, then padding is applied to the right side.
%.20c	No	None	20 characters	Displays the logger name. If the name is more than 20 characters long, then it is truncated from the beginning.
%20.30c	No	20 characters	30 characters	Displays the logger name. If the name is less than 20 characters, then padding is applied to the left side; if the name is more than 30 characters, then it is truncated from the beginning.
%-20.30c	Yes	20 characters	30 characters	Displays the logger name. If the name is shorter than 20 characters, then padding is applied to the right side to keep it left-justified. If the name is longer than 30 characters, then it is truncated from the beginning.

To illustrate the power of the conversion patterns, let's try to use LayoutDemo.java (Listing 4-1) and pass it to the following configuration file. The configuration will specify PatternLayout as the Layout object used with the ConsoleAppender, and we will pass an appropriate conversion pattern to PatternLayout.

```
#configuring the custom logger
log4j.logger.com.apress.logging.log4j=DEBUG,CONSOLE

log4j.appender.CONSOLE=org.apache.log4j.ConsoleAppender

log4j.appender.CONSOLE.layout=org.apache.log4j.PatternLayout
log4j.appender.CONSOLE.layout.ConversionPattern=%d{yyyy-MM-dd}-%t-%x-%-5p-%-
10c:%m%n
```

Executing the program with this configuration file will produce the following output to the console:

```
2002-10-20-main-22.0-INFO -com.apress.logging.log4j:The sqrt value:
4.69041575982343
2002-10-20-main-44.0-INFO -com.apress.logging.log4j:The sqrt value:
6.6332495807108
```

Now that you understand conversion patterns, you should be able to tell that the conversion pattern %r [%t] %p %c %x - %m%n means nothing other than TTCCLayout.

▓**Note** PatternLayout can be assigned to any appender regardless of the configuration style. It can be applied to a properties file or an XML-style configuration.

Conclusion

In this chapter, I have discussed in detail how each Layout object behaves and to configure these objects through a configuration file. The log4j API provides a comprehensive set of Layout objects, which is sufficient for most applications. If your application needs a more sophisticated Layout object, you must create one for yourself. You will see how to write a new Layout object in Chapter 6. In the next chapter, you will see a complete example of using log4j in a real-life application.

CHAPTER 5

■■■

Filtering, Error Handling, and Special Rendering of Log Messages

In previous chapters, we have dealt with three main components of Apache log4j: Logger, Appender, and Layout. In this chapter, you will learn how to filter the logging messages by applying different filtering criteria. You will also learn about specialized error handling mechanisms and examine how to translate application-specific domain objects to a format that log4j understands.

Filtering Explained

The process of making decisions about printing the logging information associated with each logging request is known as filtering. The decision whether to accept or reject a particular logging request can be made at several stages of the logging process. Typically, the application developer can decide whether to log certain information and reject the rest. In log4j, the filtering of log requests can be based on the level or any other application-specific criteria.

The Filter objects help to filter logging requests by analyzing the information encapsulated within the LoggingEvent object. org.apache.log4j.spi.Filter is an abstract class and the base class for all other Filter objects that can be present within the log4j framework. It defines an abstract method, public int decide(LoggingEvent event), that all the Filter subclasses override. The decide() method does the analysis on the LoggingEvent object and returns an integer value indicating the result of the analysis. The Filter objects are organized sequentially in a linear chain, and they are invoked sequentially. It is possible to add or remove any Filter object from the chain.

The filtering process within log4j typically follows these steps:

1. The application makes a logging request by invoking one of the logging methods of the Logger object.

2. The Logger object internally constructs a LoggingEvent object by encapsulating the logging message and other logging-related information.

3. The Logger object passes the LoggingEvent object to any Appender object associated with it.

4. The `Appender` object passes the `LoggingEvent` object to any of the `Filter` objects associated with it.

5. The `Filter` objects decide on the validity of the logging request based on any predefined criteria and return an integer value indicating the result of the analysis. Each `Filter` object can return three integer values:

   • If the integer value `Filter.DENY` is returned, the logging request is stopped without passing it to any other `Filter` object in the chain.

   • If the integer value `Filter.ACCEPT` is returned, the logging request is accepted, and logging information is published without consulting any other `Filter` in the chain.

   • If the integer value `Filter.NEUTRAL` is returned, the next `Filter` in the chain is consulted.

6. If there are no more `Filter` objects in the chain, the log event is logged.

The `Filter` objects are configurable only through `DOMConfigurator`. However, the `PropertyConfigurator` object does not support `DOMConfigurator`, which means these objects can be configured only through an XML configuration file, not a properties-style configuration file. But it is possible to instantiate a `Filter` object and add it to the filter chain using the `addFilter(Filter filter)` method of any `Appender` object.

One important aspect of well-designed logging code is the control over what gets produced as the final logging information. In large application scenarios, there is always a chance that the amount of information being logged is enormous. In such situations, normal level-based filtering may become inadequate to restrict logging information to exactly the type required to analyze the system. This is when `Filter` objects become very useful. They are capable of filtering out logging information based on some application-specific, complex criteria that is more business logic–specific. Apache log4j offers the flexibility of attaching any application-specific `Filter` object to the framework. With these `Filter` objects in place, we can control the logging information being produced in a more application- and business-specific way.

Level-Based Filtering

There are two ways to filter a logging request. One is to perform level-based checking against a `Logger` or `Appender` object, and the other is to attach a `Filter` object to the `Appender` objects. Level-based checking is limited to comparing the level of a logging request with the designated level of the corresponding `Logger` and `Appender` objects. A `Filter` object, however, can check a logging request against any application-specific criteria. We can write any sort of `Filter` object we want and add it to a filter chain of the `Appender` object. The filters get executed sequentially in the chain, and depending on the approval or disapproval of the logging request, the log messages are processed.

The level-based filtering that the `Logger` and `Appender` objects apply is simple in principle. If a logging request falls below the level of the `Logger` and the `Appender` object, the logging request is discarded. This is useful. But what happens if we want only logging messages belonging to a certain level or levels to print and the rest to be discarded? For example, we might want only messages with levels between `DEBUG` and `WARN` to be printed. If we set the logger level to `DEBUG`, the logger will print all the messages up to the level `FATAL`. This is the situation in which `org.apache.log4j.varia.LevelRangeFilter` comes into play.

Using LevelRangeFilter

With LevelRangeFilter, we can specify the lower range and the upper range of logging levels that the logging framework should approve. LevelRangeFilter has the configurable bean properties listed in Table 5-1.

Table 5-1. *Bean Properties in LevelRangeFilter*

Bean Property	Method	Description	Default
LevelMin	setLevelMin(Level)	Sets the minimum level to consider for logging	None
LevelMax	setLevelMax(Level)	Sets the maximum level for which the logging request should be handled	None
AcceptOnMatch	SetAcceptOnMatch(boolean)	If true, the filter returns ACCEPT, and the next filters in the chain will not be considered	false

The Filter objects are currently configurable via an XML configuration file only. Listing 5-1, customFilter.xml, is a sample configuration file that uses LevelRangeFilter.

Listing 5-1. *customFilter.xml*

```xml
<?xml version="1.0" encoding="UTF-8"?>
<!DOCTYPE log4j:configuration SYSTEM "log4j.dtd">

<log4j:configuration xmlns:log4j="http://jakarta.apache.org/log4j/">

 <appender name="A1" class="org.apache.log4j.ConsoleAppender">

   <layout class="org.apache.log4j.PatternLayout">
     <param name="ConversionPattern" value="%t %-5p %c{2} - %m%n"/>
   </layout>

   <filter class="org.apache.log4j.varia.LevelRangeFilter">
     <param name="LevelMin" value="DEBUG"/>
     <param name="LevelMax" value="WARN"/>
     <param name="acceptOnMatch" value="true"/>

   </filter>
 </appender>

<logger name="com.apress.logging.log4j">
   <level value="debug"/>
   <appender-ref ref="A1"/>
</logger>

</log4j:configuration>
```

Notice that in this configuration file, we assign a `PatternLayout` to the `ConsoleAppender` object. `ConsoleAppender` also uses the `LevelRangeFilter` object with the minimum logging level set as `DEBUG` and the maximum logging level set as `WARN`. The `acceptOnMatch` property is set to `true`. This means that if an event's level is within the specified range, the event will be logged straightaway without consulting any more `Filter` objects in the chain. If `acceptOnMatch` is set to `false`, it means that `Filter.NEUTRAL` will be returned even if the event level is within the specified range. This gives the other `Filter` objects in the chain an opportunity to inspect the event.

Now we will write a simple program to demonstrate how `LevelRangeFilter` works. Listing 5-2, `FilterDemo.java`, is a sample program that prints logging messages with all the levels. With the help of `LevelRangeFilter`, we will filter out any message that is not within the range of the `DEBUG` and `WARN` levels.

Listing 5-2. *FilterDemo.java*

```
package com.apress.logging.log4j;

import org.apache.log4j.Logger;
public class FilterDemo
{
    private static Logger logger =
Logger.getLogger(FilterDemo.class.getPackage().getName());

    public FilterDemo()
    {
    }
    public void doLogging()
    {
        logger.debug("DEBUG MESSAGE..");
        logger.info("INFO MESSAGE..");
        logger.error("ERROR MESSAGE..");
        logger.warn("WARN MESSAGE..");
        logger.fatal("FATAL MESSAGE...");
    }

    public static void main(String args[])
    {
        FilterDemo demo = new FilterDemo();
        demo.doLogging();
    }

}
```

Executing this program will print all the messages to the console except the messages with levels `ERROR` and `FATAL`, as they fall outside the range specified.

```
main DEBUG logging.log4j - DEBUG MESSAGE..
main INFO  logging.log4j - INFO MESSAGE..
main WARN  logging.log4j - WARN MESSAGE..
```

▓**Note** Recall that the logging level sequence is ALL<DEBUG<INFO<WARN<ERROR<FATAL<OFF.

As you can see, assigning a level to the Logger objects and a threshold level to the Appender objects can always restrict the lower range of the level. LevelRangeFilter becomes useful only when we want to restrict the upper range of the level.

Matching a Particular Level—LevelMatchFilter

This Filter compares the level associated with the internally generated LoggingEvent with the one specified in the configuration of this Filter. The LevelMatchFilter has two configurable properties: levelToMatch and acceptOnMatch. If the acceptOnMatch property of the LevelMatchFilter is set to true, it returns ACCEPT upon finding a LoggingEvent with a matching level. If acceptOnMatch is set to false, it returns DENY. If there is no match, it returns NEUTRAL.

Matching a String—StringMatchFilter

This Filter compares the message in the LoggingEvent with the specified stringToMatch property. It also has two configurable properties: stringToMatch and acceptOnMatch. If acceptOnMatch is set to true, it returns ACCEPT upon finding an exact matching String. If it is false, it returns DENY. If there is no match, NEUTRAL is returned.

A Custom Level-Based Filter—SelectedLevelFilter

You have seen how LevelRangeFilter can help set upper and lower bounds for logging levels. In another situation, we might want to have a Filter that allows only messages with specified levels to appear in the destination. This is more precise than specifying a range of levels. For example, in one scenario, we might want only the messages with levels FATAL and INFO to be printed. One immediate solution is to write a custom Filter object to handle such situations.

We will now explore a sample Filter object designed to filter messages based on specific levels. The SelectedLevelFilter class extends the abstract class org.apache.log4j.spi.Filter and implements the abstract method decide(LoggingEvent event) to determine a certain logging event.

SelectedLevelFilter defines two configurable bean properties:

- The acceptOnMatch property defines whether the filter should accept this request if a matching criterion is found. If a matching level is found and acceptOnMatch is set to true, it returns Filter.ACCEPT. If a matching level is found and acceptOnMatch is set to false, it returns Filter.NEUTRAL. If no level match is found, the acceptOnMatch property is ignored and it returns Filter.DENY.

- The levelsToMatch property accepts a comma-delimited string representation of levels we want to match. For example, if we wanted to find messages with the levels DEBUG and FATAL, we would define levelsToMatch as DEBUG,FATAL. The sequence in which the levels are specified is immaterial here.

At initialization, the SelectedLevelFilter object stores all the specified levels in the levelsToMatch parameter in an internal java.util.ArrayList object. When a logging event arrives, it compares its level against all those specified with levelsToMatch. SelectedLevelFilter then returns an appropriate return value—Filter.ACCEPT, Filter.DENY, or Filter.NEUTRAL—depending on the result of the comparison and the value of acceptOnMatch.

Listing 5-3, SelectedLevelFilter.java, presents a sample implementation of the custom Filter object discussed in this section.

Listing 5-3. *SelectedLevelFilter.java*

```
package com.apress.logging.log4j;

import org.apache.log4j.spi.Filter;
import org.apache.log4j.spi.LoggingEvent;
import org.apache.log4j.Level;
import org.apache.log4j.helpers.OptionConverter;
import java.util.ArrayList;
import java.util.Iterator;
import java.util.StringTokenizer;

public class SelectedLevelFilter extends Filter {
    private ArrayList levels = new ArrayList();
    private boolean acceptOnMatch;
    private String levelsToMatch;

    public SelectedLevelFilter() {
    }

    public int decide(LoggingEvent event)
    {
        if(levels.size() == 0)
        {
            return Filter.NEUTRAL;
        }
        Level eventLevel = event.getLevel();
        Iterator iterator = levels.iterator();
        boolean matchFound = false;

        while(iterator.hasNext())
        {
            Level level = (Level)iterator.next();
            if(level.equals(eventLevel))
            {
                matchFound = true;
                break;
            }
        }
```

```
        if(matchFound)
        {
            if(acceptOnMatch)
            {
                return Filter.ACCEPT;
            }else
            {
                return Filter.NEUTRAL;
            }
        }else
        {
            return Filter.DENY;
        }
    }

    public boolean getAcceptOnMatch() {
        return this.acceptOnMatch;
    }

    public void setAcceptOnMatch(boolean acceptOnMatch) {
        this.acceptOnMatch = acceptOnMatch;
    }

    public String getLevelsToMatch() {
        return this.levelsToMatch;
    }

    public void setLevelsToMatch(String levelsToMatch) {
        this.levelsToMatch = levelsToMatch;
        if(levelsToMatch !=null)
        {
            StringTokenizer tokenizer = new StringTokenizer(levelsToMatch,
",");
            while(tokenizer.hasMoreTokens())
            {
                String token = tokenizer.nextToken().trim();
                Level level = OptionConverter.toLevel(token, null);
                levels.add(level);
            }
        }

    }

}
```

Let's reuse the program FilterDemo.java from Listing 5-2 to demonstrate the application of SelectedLevelFilter. As the Filter objects can be configured only with an XML configuration file, we will also reuse the configuration file customFilter.xml shown in Listing 5-1. Make the following changes to the `<filter>` attribute in the XML file to specify `SelectedLevelFilter` as the designated filter for the defined logger:

```
<filter class="com.apress.logging.log4j.SelectedLevelFilter">
    <param name="LevelsToMatch" value="FATAL,INFO"/>
    <param name="acceptOnMatch" value="true"/>
</filter>
```

In the `levelsToMatch` property, we specify levels `FATAL` and `INFO` as the desired levels for the messages to be published. Now execute the `FilterDemo` program with the changed configuration file. Only the messages with level `FATAL` and `INFO` will be printed to the console.

```
main INFO  logging.log4j - INFO MESSAGE..
main FATAL logging.log4j - FATAL MESSAGE...
```

Filter Chaining

The Apache log4j API provides many `Filter` objects targeted for different purposes. As you have seen, if a particular `Filter` object returns a value of `Filter.NEUTRAL`, then the next filter in the chain is considered. This is called filter chaining. By chaining several `Filter` objects, we can compare a particular logging request against many filtering conditions. Sometimes, this serves as the alternative to writing a custom `Filter` object to combine the features offered by different `Filter` objects. For instance, the previous example of filtering messages only with levels `FATAL` and `INFO` can be achieved by chaining two instances of `LevelMatchFilter`. Let's see what happens when we replace the configuration file in Listing 5-1 with the one in Listing 5-4.

Listing 5-4. *Another Filter Configuration File*

```
<?xml version="1.0" encoding="UTF-8"?>
<!DOCTYPE log4j:configuration SYSTEM "log4j.dtd">

<log4j:configuration xmlns:log4j="http://jakarta.apache.org/log4j/">

 <appender name="A1" class="org.apache.log4j.ConsoleAppender">

   <layout class="org.apache.log4j.PatternLayout">
     <param name="ConversionPattern" value="%t %-5p %c{2} - %m%n"/>
   </layout>

  <filter class="org.apache.log4j.varia.LevelMatchFilter">
     <param name="levelToMatch" value="FATAL"/>
     <param name="acceptOnMatch" value="true"/>
   </filter>

  <filter class="org.apache.log4j.varia.LevelMatchFilter">
     <param name="levelToMatch" value="INFO"/>
     <param name="acceptOnMatch" value="true"/>
   </filter>
```

```
    <filter class="org.apache.log4j.varia.DenyAllFilter"/>
</appender>

<logger name="com.apress.logging.log4j">
    <level value="debug"/>
    <appender-ref ref="A1"/>
</logger>

</log4j:configuration>
```

LevelMatchFilter has two configuration properties: levelToMatch and acceptOnMatch. We use two instances of LevelMatchFilter to filter out messages with level FATAL and INFO only. The most important entry is the last filter in the chain. DenyAllFilter is there to deny all logging requests previously dealt with by other appenders in the chain with the return value Filter. NEUTRAL. If the acceptOnMatch property is set to true, the LevelMatchFilter object returns Filter. NEUTRAL if it finds no match. If it does find a match, then Filter.ACCEPT is returned and the logging event is logged. All the mismatched logging events then end up in DenyAllFilter, and it consumes all these mismatched events without printing them.

▓**Caution** Do not forget to add DenyAllFilter at the end of the chain to ignore all messages not matching the criteria.

Error Handling

However robust an application's code is, it is virtually impossible to predict and handle all potential error conditions. A good system is measured by its resilience and how efficiently an error condition is handled. So far you have seen how to log information about the internal state of an application's running instance. You have seen that with log4j, logging information can be sent out to various destinations locally or over a network. There is every chance that these operations may generate some erroneous conditions in their process of publishing logging information.

The question is what should happen when one of the logging components encounters some problem. Here are some suggestions:

- The primary application itself should not crash just because there is some problem with the logging activity.

- The logging component should handle errors internally without throwing the errors or exceptions back to the caller application. This saves the caller application from having to worry about the logging components.

- The logging components should allow the application developer flexibility in how to address such error conditions.

Apache log4j is a resilient logging framework. It takes care of all the aspects involving erroneous logging conditions. By default, the log4j Appender objects use the OnlyOnceErrorHandler object, which outputs an error message once and only once to System.err and ignores the subsequent error messages. This is graceful error handling; it does not cause the main application to crash, and the administrator can see the error message produced and try to fix the problem.

Figure 5-1 presents the different error-handling objects within log4j and their relationships. Note that all the error-handling objects implement a common interface, org.apache.log4j.spi. ErrorHandler. This interface defines the error-handling methods that are subsequently implemented in the specific error-handling objects.

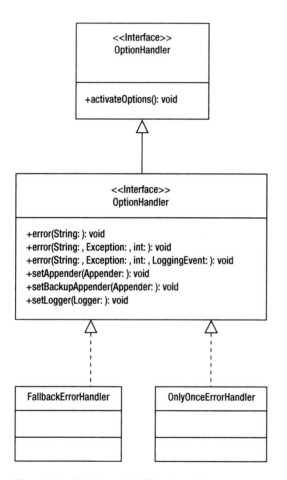

Figure 5-1. *The ErrorHandler class diagram*

The ErrorHandler interface also defines a couple of methods in addition to the error-handling methods, as shown in Table 5-2.

Table 5-2. *Methods in the ErrorHandler Interface*

Method	Description
error(String)	Handles the error by publishing the message passed to it
error(String , Exception , int)	Handles the error by publishing the error information, including the Java exception being thrown and the integer error code describing the problem
error(String , Exception , int , LoggingEvent)	Handles the error by publishing the error message, the exception, the integer error code, and the logging event that generated the error
setAppender(Appender)	Sets the appender for which the error is handled
setBackupAppender(Appender)	Sets the backup appender to fall back to in case the primary appender fails
setLogger(Logger)	Sets the reference of the logger to which the failing appender might be attached

Apache log4j by default provides two error-handling objects:

- org.apache.log4j.helpers.OnlyOnceErrorHandler: This is the default error handler used within log4j Appender objects. It prints the error message from the appender once and only once to System.err and ignores subsequent error messages.

▨**Note** OnlyOnceErrorHandler works per Appender object. If for some reasons two NullPointerExceptions are thrown due to some problem, only the first one will be printed to System.err and the second one will be ignored if the Appender is using onlyOnceErrorHandler. It does not matter whether the exception is thrown from the same place or different places within the application.

- org.apache.log4j.varia.FallbackErrorHandler: This error handler also prints error messages to System.err. In addition, it can configure a secondary appender to be the backup appender for all the loggers that use FallbackErrorHandler. This means that when the first error arrives, it iterates through all the logger references associated with the primary appender defined as a part of the FallbackErrorHandler configuration. For each of the Logger objects found, it removes their primary appenders and sets the backup appender as the primary appender. This ensures that subsequent logging requests will now be directed to the backup appender, and that no further error conditions arise due to the appender operation.

You won't always be happy with the default log4j error handling. For example, you might not be happy about producing error messages to a console when you really want to redirect all logging events to use a different appender to send information to a secondary destination. Say you are using JDBCAppender to log information to a database, and the database goes down while your application is still running. What do you want to do now? You may want to log the error report and then continue logging information in a file instead. You can write your own custom error handler to do the job and configure log4j to use your custom error handler.

ErrorCode Interface

To identify errors in a systematic way, log4j allocates error codes to different types of errors. These are encapsulated within the ErrorCode interface. The error codes are used within an Appender object to pass generated errors to the appropriate ErrorHandler class attached to the Appender. We can extend this interface to define our own error codes in case we need them.

Writing a Custom ErrorHandler

Let's write a custom error handler object. We want this custom error handler to achieve the following:

- Implement the ErrorHandler interface.

- Accept a logger reference.

- Accept an appender reference.

- The appender reference identifies the backup appender that will handle the error condition. The logger reference identifies the logger to which the specified Appender is attached.

- Keep a reference to all the loggers specified as having the primary Appender object associated with them.

- In the error condition, remove the primary appender from the loggers specified and set the backup Appender object to be the primary appender thereafter.

Listing 5-5, CustomErrorHandler.java, is designed to do the jobs iterated in the bulleted list. This is a very simple error handler. The implementation of error(message, exception, errorCode, LoggingEvent) does the bulk of the work.

Listing 5-5. *CustomErrorHandler.java*

```
package com.apress.logging.log4j;

import org.apache.log4j.spi.ErrorHandler;
import org.apache.log4j.spi.LoggingEvent;
import org.apache.log4j.Logger;
import org.apache.log4j.Appender;

import java.util.Vector;

public class CustomErrorHandler implements ErrorHandler
{
    private Appender primary;
    private Appender backup;
    private Vector loggers = new Vector();

    public CustomErrorHandler()
    {

    }
```

```java
    public void activateOptions()
    {

    }

    public void setLogger(Logger logger)
    {
        if (logger != null)
        {
            loggers.add(logger);
        }
    }

    public void error(String message, Exception e, int errorCode)
    {
        error(message, e, errorCode, null);
    }

    public void error(String message)
    {
        error(message, null, 0, null);
    }

    public void error(String message, Exception e, int errorCode,
LoggingEvent event)
    {
        for (int i = 0; i < loggers.size(); i++)
        {
            Logger l = (Logger) loggers.elementAt(i);
            l.removeAppender(primary);
            l.addAppender(backup);
            l.error(message, e);
        }

    }

    public void setAppender(Appender appender)
    {
        this.primary = appender;
    }

    public void setBackupAppender(Appender appender)
    {
        this.backup = appender;
    }
}
```

Configuring ErrorHandler

At the moment in log4j, error handlers can be configured only via an XML-style configuration file or programmatically. Here we will use the XML-style configuration, as it is more flexible than the hard-coded programmatic configuration. Listing 5-6, errorHandler.xml, shows the code for the sample configuration file.

Listing 5-6. *errorHandler.xml*

```
<?xml version="1.0" encoding="UTF-8"?>
<!DOCTYPE log4j:configuration SYSTEM "log4j.dtd">

<log4j:configuration xmlns:log4j="http://jakarta.apache.org/log4j/">

 <appender name="FILE" class="org.apache.log4j.FileAppender">
    <param name="file" value="${user.home}/backup.log"/>
    <param name="append" value="true"/>

    <layout class="org.apache.log4j.SimpleLayout"/>

 </appender>

 <appender name="JDBC" class="org.apache.log4j.jdbc.JDBCAppender">

   <errorHandler class="com.apress.logging.log4j.CustomErrorHandler">
    <logger-ref ref="com.apress.logging.log4j"/>
    <appender-ref ref="FILE"/>
   </errorHandler>

   <param name="URL" value="jdbc:odbc:dbdef"/>
   <param name="user" value="system"/>
   <param name="password" value="manager"/>
   <param name="sql" value="INSERT INTO LOGGING_DATA VALUES('%x','%d{yyyy-MM-
dd}','%C','%p','%m')"/>

 </appender>

 <logger name="com.apress.logging.log4j">
    <level value="debug"/>
    <appender-ref ref="JDBC"/>
 </logger>
</log4j:configuration>
```

The errorHandler element is defined as a child element of the appender named JDBCelement. This means that the defined error handler will be used in connection with the appender named JDBC. The JDBC appender writes the data to the database by using the configuration parameters defined.

In this sample configuration, the error handler is set to the custom error handler com.apress. logging.log4j.CustomErrorHandler. CustomErrorHandler is defined as a child element to the

JDBC appender. This means that the primary appender for CustomErrorHandler is set to be the JDBC appender.

The logger-ref element defines the logger that is using the appender JDBC. The appender-ref element defines the backup appender for the JDBC appender. In this example, the backup appender is FILE. The FILE appender, in turn, is configured to be org.apache.log4j.FileAppender.

Finally, the configuration of the FILE appender indicates that the logging information will be directed to the backup.log file in the user.home directory.

Running the Example

Running the example is very simple. To see CustomErrorHandler at work, change the database configuration parameters in the configuration file errorHandler.xml (Listing 5-6) to some invalid values. This will cause the JDBCAppender to fail. This is when CustomErrorHandler will take charge and do the backup job. Finally, go to the user.home directory to check what is written in the backup.log file.

ObjectRenderer

The logging information that we intend to publish can be of various types and in various formats. Typically, in an object-oriented application where several objects hold data and interact with each other, we need to publish whole objects and their contents in a human-readable format. Inspecting the current status of the object and the attribute values a particular object holds makes it easier to understand how that object is behaving in response to certain messages sent to it. It also makes it possible to define the corrective actions required in case the object is not behaving appropriately.

In the context of log4j, a Logger class has several logging methods, all of which can accept an Object argument as the logging message. This Object argument can be a simple String representing the exact text information we wish to publish or a custom Object such as a Customer, a Person, etc. When we pass a custom Object to be logged, the intention is to publish the state and the content of the object. The org.apache.log4j.or.ObjectRenderer interface defines the way to associate any ObjectRenderer with any Object and obtain a String representation of the content of the object.

Layout objects call the ObjectRenderer to obtain a String representation of the Object content before they attempt to format the Object argument passed to the Logger. If the message argument passed to the Logger is a String, no ObjectRenderer is required to convert the message, and the Layout object processes the message.

The ObjectRenderer objects can be configured only with DOMConfigurator and thereby can be defined in an XML-style configuration file. The configuration information of an ObjectRenderer defines the rendering class, which is an implementation of the org.apache.log4j.or.ObjectRenderer interface, and defines the rendered class, which is the custom Object that needs to be rendered as a String representation.

A Custom Renderer Example

Let us consider a hypothetical domain object presented in Listing 5-7. This represents a customer order. We want to log this CustomerOrder object using log4j. For this purpose, we will develop a specific Renderer object, which will translate a given instance of CustomerOrder to a log4j-understandable message.

Listing 5-7. *CustomerOrder.java*

```java
package com.apress.business;

public class CustomerOrder {

    /** Holds value of property productName. */
    private String productName;

    /** Holds value of property productCode. */
    private int productCode;

    /** Holds value of property productPrice. */
    private int productPrice;

    /** Creates a new instance of CustomerOrder */
    public CustomerOrder() {
    }

    public CustomerOrder(String name, int code, int price)
    {
        this.productCode = code;
        this.productPrice = price;
        this.productName = name;
    }


    /** Getter for property productName.
     * @return Value of property productName.
     */
    public String getProductName() {
        return this.productName;
    }

    /** Setter for property productName.
     * @param productName New value of property productName.
     */
    public void setProductName(String productName) {
        this.productName = productName;
    }

    /** Getter for property productCode.
     * @return Value of property productCode.
     */
    public int getProductCode() {
        return this.productCode;
    }
```

```java
/** Setter for property productCode.
 * @param productCode New value of property productCode.
 */
public void setProductCode(int productCode) {
    this.productCode = productCode;
}

/** Getter for property productPrice.
 * @return Value of property productPrice.
 */
public int getProductPrice() {
    return this.productPrice;
}

/** Setter for property productPrice.
 * @param productPrice New value of property productPrice.
 */
public void setProductPrice(int productPrice) {
    this.productPrice = productPrice;
}
}
```

The program in Listing 5-8, OrderRenderer.java, implements the ObjectRenderer interface and provides an implementation of the doRender(Object obj) method. To keep the example simple, it returns a hyphen-separated list of the attribute values of the CustomerOrder object.

Listing 5-8. *OrderRenderer.java*

```java
package com.apress.logging.log4j.renderer;

import org.apache.log4j.or.ObjectRenderer;
import com.apress.business.CustomerOrder;

public class OrderRenderer implements ObjectRenderer
{
    private static final String separator = "-";

    /** Creates a new instance of OrderRenderer */
    public OrderRenderer() {
    }

    public String doRender(Object obj)
    {
        StringBuffer buffer = new StringBuffer(50);
        CustomerOrder order = null;
        String productName = null;
        int productCode = 0;
        int productPrice = 0;
```

```
        //check if the instance is of correct type CustomerOrder
        if(obj instanceof CustomerOrder)
        {
            order = (CustomerOrder)obj;
            productName = order.getProductName();
            productCode = order.getProductCode();
            productPrice = order.getProductPrice();

            buffer.append(productName);
            buffer.append(separator);
            buffer.append(new Integer(productCode).toString());
            buffer.append(separator);
            buffer.append(new Integer(productPrice).toString());
        }

        return buffer.toString();
    }
}
```

Configuring ObjectRenderer

Now, once we have all the objects ready, we need to pass the object hierarchy to the log4j framework. As discussed before, the ObjectRenderer can be configured only through DOMConfigurator, and we will define the logger configuration through an XML-style configuration file. Listing 5-9 shows the configuration file used for this example, renderer_properties.xml.

Listing 5-9. *renderer_properties.xml*

```
<?xml version="1.0" encoding="UTF-8"?>
<!DOCTYPE log4j:configuration SYSTEM "log4j.dtd">

<log4j:configuration xmlns:log4j="http://jakarta.apache.org/log4j/">

 <renderer renderedClass="com.apress.business.CustomerOrder"
renderingClass="com.apress.logging.log4j.renderer.OrderRenderer">
 </renderer>

 <appender name="A1" class="org.apache.log4j.ConsoleAppender">

   <layout class="org.apache.log4j.PatternLayout">
     <param name="ConversionPattern" value="%t %-5p %c{2} - %m%n"/>
   </layout>
</appender>

 <logger name="com.apress.logging.log4j">
   <level value="debug"/>
   <appender-ref ref="A1"/>
 </logger>
</log4j:configuration>
```

Renderer in Action

Finally, Listing 5-10 presents a sample application to demonstrate rendering of the CustomerOrder object.

Listing 5-10. *ProductRendererDemo.java*

```java
package com.apress.logging.log4j;

import org.apache.log4j.Logger;
import com.apress.business.CustomerOrder;
import com.apress.logging.log4j.filter.ProductFilter;
import com.apress.logging.log4j.renderer.OrderRenderer;
public class ProductRendererDemo
{
    private static Logger logger =
Logger.getLogger(ProductRendererDemo.class.getPackage().getName());

    /** Creates a new instance of ProductRendererDemo */
    public ProductRendererDemo () {
    }

    public void processOrder(CustomerOrder order)
    {
        logger.info(order);
    }

    public static void main(String args[])
    {
        CustomerOrder order1 = new CustomerOrder("Beer", 101, 20);
        CustomerOrder order2 = new CustomerOrder("Chocolate", 223, 5);

        ProductRendererDemo demo = new ProductRendererDemo();
        demo.processOrder(order1);
        demo.processOrder(order2);
    }

}
```

This application creates three different CustomerOrder objects with different product names, product codes, and product prices. The processOrder() method simply logs the CustomerOrder object passed to it. With the ProductFilter object in place, executing the application in Listing 5-10 will result in the following log messages being printed, excluding any products that have product codes below 100:

```
main INFO  logging.log4j - Beer-101-20
main INFO  logging.log4j - Chocolate-223-5
```

What Is Formatting and What Is Rendering?

At this stage, the difference between rendering and formatting (as discussed in Chapter 4) may need a little bit more clarification. The primary goal of rendering is to represent the object we are trying to log in a loggable format. Renderer often does a job similar to the toString() method. However, Renderers are capable of doing a lot more in terms of application-specific representation of the state of an object, whereas toString() can potentially be used in other areas of the application and better be kept separate and simplistic.

Layout objects, on the other hand, have more to do with how to format the logging messages as a whole. Layout objects can deal with custom objects rendered by using custom Renderer objects and then publish the whole logging information to the final destination.

Conclusion

In this chapter, you have learned about filtering, error handling, and object rendering in Apache log4j. These are powerful techniques to tailor the final logging output according to the application software's requirements. In complex application scenarios, these techniques become very useful for controlling the amount of logging information published and organizing it in such a way that it can be processed to generate reports for different functional aspects of an organization.

Extending log4j to Create Custom Logging Components

In the previous chapters, we covered the core log4j framework. We have discussed how the Logger, Appender, Layout, and Filter objects interact with each other and publish logging information to a preferred destination. Apache log4j offers a vast range of Appender objects. These give us the power to publish logging data to a local machine and to distribute logging data over a network. Moreover, the flexible and highly configurable nature of log4j allows us to change logging behavior completely by merely changing the configuration file.

All this is great and useful. Still, there may be situations in which the default log4j capabilities do not quite fit a sophisticated application's requirements. In such situations, we have to extend the log4j framework to devise our own logging components to meet our application's requirements.

In this chapter, you will learn how to extend the log4j framework to create custom application-specific components.

Why We Need Custom Logging Components

Log4j is a feature-rich logging framework. However, each real-life application is unique and default features within log4j might fall short of the requirements of a particular application. You may need to create new Appender objects publishing logging information to new destinations, or you may need to view the logging information in a certain way. In the following example, you will see how to view the logging information in a separate window-based control.

You might think, What is the use of this window-based log viewer? One scenario could be to allow users to view the logging information in real time. Another way to achieve a real-time log view is to use the tail utility of the UNIX operating system. This type of Appender object could also be useful if you are not interested in storing the log messages or do not have a console to print the logging information.

Creating the Custom WindowAppender

In this section, we'll explore how you can create your own Appender objects. You may want Java window-based logging in an application so you can monitor log information in some sort of GUI control. This means that the Logger objects in an application should be configured to send logging information to a Java window. To achieve this, you can create a custom appender named WindowAppender that is capable of printing all logging information to a small Java-based window.

Features of the Custom WindowAppender

As mentioned in Chapter 3, these objects all inherit from a base class called `AppenderSkeleton`. Any custom `Appender` object must adhere to this appender hierarchy. The log4j framework checks for this criterion before invoking any appender specified and ignores any that do not adhere to the hierarchy.

Sticking to the appender hierarchy makes it fairly easy to write custom `Appender` objects. In this example, we will create a `WindowAppender` object. Before writing the code for the `WindowAppender` object, let's take a look at the features we will include:

- The `WindowAppender` will create a small Java `Frame`-based window.

- The window will display logging information in a scrollable area.

- The `title`, `width`, and `height` properties of the window should be configurable through bean properties.

The Bottlenecks

This looks simple, but be aware of a few bottlenecks with this `WindowAppender`. We need to decide how different `Logger` objects within any application will access `WindowAppender`. The following points are important to consider before we create the `WindowAppender` object:

- An application may have several `Logger` objects, and each of them may try to use the `WindowAppender` object to log information.

- We need to make sure that for all the created instances of `WindowAppender` one and only one window is active.

- If for every `Logger` object using the `WindowAppender` object a separate logging window is created, the system will soon be full of logging windows, which is not desirable.

The Custom WindowAppender Architecture

Considering the features we need to provide and the bottlenecks we should be aware of, we need to find a way to create a single instance of the logging window and make it available to all instances of `WindowAppender`. The best time to create the logging window is when the appender is initialized.

Let's go through the appender initialization process:

- If the appender configuration is specified in a configuration file, the log4j framework will read the appender configuration from that file.

- The log4j framework first creates an instance of the specified `Appender` class by calling the default constructor of that class.

- If other bean properties are specified in the configuration file, the `set()` methods of the corresponding bean property are invoked to set the property values.

- Finally, the `activateOptions()` method of the specified `Appender` class is invoked to initialize any optional configuration for the appender. This method is optional to any appender and therefore may or may not be present in a particular `Appender` object.

Let's turn our attention back to `WindowAppender`. Where is the best place to initialize the logging window? Because we have the bean properties to set the `title`, `height`, and `width` attributes of the logging window, we cannot create an instance of the logging window before the initialization process sets these bean properties. Thus, the best place to create an instance of the logging window is in the activateOptions() method after the bean properties are set.

Also, we need to make sure that no more than one instance of the logging window gets created. So we should move the creation and instantiation of the logging window to a synchronized method to return a static singleton instance of the logging window.

Implementing the Custom WindowAppender

Listing 6-1 demonstrates WindowAppender.java, the custom window-based Appender object.

Listing 6-1. *WindowAppender.java*

```
package com.apress.logging.log4j.appender;

import org.apache.log4j.AppenderSkeleton;
import org.apache.log4j.spi.LoggingEvent;
import javax.swing.JFrame;
import javax.swing.JTextArea;
import javax.swing.JScrollPane;

/** This is a custom Appender object publishing the logging
 * information to a Java window. The logging Java window is a
 * singleton instance across all the instances of this Appender
 * object.
 */
public class WindowAppender extends AppenderSkeleton{

    private static JFrame frame = null;
    private static JTextArea area = null;
    private static JScrollPane pane = null;

    /** Holds value of property title. */
    private static String title;

    /** Holds value of property height. */
    private static int height;

    /** Holds value of property width. */
    private static int width;

    /** Creates a new instance of WindowAppender */
    public WindowAppender() {
    }
    /**
     *This method is called as a part of the appender initialization process
     */
```

```java
    public void activateOptions() {
        getWindowInstance();
    }
    /**
     * private method to initialize the logging window
     */
    private synchronized JFrame getWindowInstance() {
        area = new JTextArea();
        pane = new JScrollPane(area);
        if(frame == null) {
            frame = new JFrame(title);
            frame.setSize(width,height);
            frame.getContentPane().add(pane);
            frame.setVisible(true);
        }
        return frame;
    }


    /** This method is overridden from the super class and
     * prints the logging message to the logging window.
     * NOTE: If there is no layout specified for this Appender,
     * no message will be displayed. The logging information is
     * formatted according to the layout and the conversion pattern
     * specified.
     * @param loggingEvent encapsulates the logging information.
     */
    protected void append(LoggingEvent loggingEvent) {
        //simply extract the message and display it
        JScrollPane pane =
(JScrollPane)frame.getContentPane().getComponent(0);
        JTextArea area = (JTextArea)pane.getViewport().getView();
        if(this.layout !=null) {
            area.append(this.layout.format(loggingEvent));
        }
    }

    /** This method is overridden from the super class and disposes
     * the logging window.
     */
    public void close() {
        frame.dispose();
    }

    /** This method is overridden from the super class and always
     * returns true to indicate that a Layout is required for
     * this appender. If not specified in the conf. file, then it
     * will not print any message in the log window.
     */
```

```java
public boolean requiresLayout() {
    return true;
}

/** Getter for property title.
 * @return Value of property title.
 */
public String getTitle() {
    return this.title;
}|

/** Setter for property title.
 * @param title New value of property title.
 */
public void setTitle(String title) {
    this.title = title;
}

/** Getter for property height.
 * @return Value of property height.
 */
public int getHeight() {
    return this.height;
}

/** Setter for property height.
 * @param height New value of property height.
 */
public void setHeight(int height) {
    this.height = height;
}

/** Getter for property width.
 * @return Value of property width.
 */
public int getWidth() {
    return this.width;
}

/** Setter for property width.
 * @param width New value of property width.
 */
public void setWidth(int width) {
    this.width = width;
}

}
```

As we can see in this WindowAppender, getWindowInstance() is a private synchronized method responsible for creating a JFrame instance with the specified title, width, and height bean properties. We have provided an overridden append() method that writes logging data to the JTextArea embedded within a JScrollPane attached to the JFrame. Each time a logging request arrives, the logging message is printed to the JTextArea. Notice that the requiresLayout() method in WindowAppender returns true. This means WindowAppender requires a Layout object to be associated with it, and it uses the Layout object to format the logging event before displaying the message. If no Layout object is specified, no logging message will be displayed in the window. The activateOptions() method calls the getWindowInstance() method, which creates a new logging window JFrame instance or returns an already existing one.

If we are configuring programmatically, we have to explicitly call the activateOptions() method to get a logging window created. As the getWindowInstance() method is synchronized and returns one and only one instance of the JFrame object, it is protected against multiple programs calling the activateOptions() method of the WindowAppender. No matter how the configuration is done, we will always get one instance of the logging window per application instance.

Testing the Custom WindowAppender

To test WindowAppender, we will use the WindowAppender object as the appender for two separate Logger objects appearing in two different application class files. These files are shown in Listing 6-2 and Listing 6-3.

Listing 6-2, AnotherClass.java, creates a named logger, Logger2, and Listing 6-3, WindowAppenderDemo.java, creates named loggers, Logger1 and Logger2. Both of the classes perform some simple logging activity.

Listing 6-2. *AnotherClass.java*

```
package com.apress.logging.log4j.appender;

import org.apache.log4j.Logger;

public class AnotherClass {
    private static Logger logger = Logger.getLogger("Logger2");

    /** Creates a new instance of AnotherClass */
    public AnotherClass() {
    }

    public void logAnotherMessage()
    {
        logger.info("Message from Another class..");
    }
}
```

Listing 6-3. *WindowAppenderDemo.java*

```java
package com.apress.logging.log4j.appender;

import org.apache.log4j.Logger;

public class WindowAppenderDemo {

    private static Logger logger1 = Logger.getLogger("Logger1");
    private static Logger logger2 = Logger.getLogger("Logger2");

    /** Creates a new instance of WindowAppenderDemo */
    public WindowAppenderDemo() {
    }

    public void doLogging()
    {
        logger1.info("Message from logger1");
        logger2.info("Message from logger2");
    }

    /**
     * @param args the command line arguments
     */
    public static void main(String[] args) {
        WindowAppenderDemo demo = new WindowAppenderDemo();
        demo.doLogging();
        AnotherClass anc = new AnotherClass();
        anc.logAnotherMessage();
    }
}
```

When executing the program in Listing 6-3, we will see a small logging window with logging messages displayed in it, as shown in Figure 6-1.

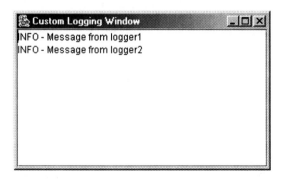

Figure 6-1. *Logging information produced by WindowAppender*

We will write a small configuration file, `customappender.properties`, to configure both of the `Logger` objects used in the example classes in Listings 6-2 and 6-3. This file, shown in Listing 6-4, exhibits the configuration to use for this example.

Listing 6-4. *customappender.properties*

```
#configuring the custom logger
log4j.logger.Logger1=DEBUG,WINDOW
log4j.logger.Logger2=DEBUG,WINDOW

#configuring the WINDOW appender
log4j.appender.WINDOW=com.apress.logging.log4j.appender.WindowAppender
log4j.appender.WINDOW.layout=org.apache.log4j.SimpleLayout
log4j.appender.WINDOW.title=Custom Logging Window
log4j.appender.WINDOW.width=200
log4j.appender.WINDOW.height=200
```

In this configuration file, we pass the values for `title`, `width`, and `height` for `WindowAppender`. We also specify `SimpleLayout` as the layout to be used by `WindowAppender`.

Configuring log4j from a Database

As we have discussed previously, one of the most important features of log4j is its highly configurable nature. We can define application-specific configuration files either in properties style or in XML style. Also, the configuration files can reside in a remote place, and we can still load configuration information provided the resource is accessible from a URL.

The fact that logging behavior can be controlled through configuration files makes it easy to change the logging style without altering the source code, instead changing configuration information or pointing the application to a different set of configuration files.

In certain application scenarios, we might prefer to control the log4j configuration information from a central database. This can give us the power to apply a centrally controlled logging style to different application components. When we put the configuration information in a database, all the components will use the same configuration file. The `Logger`, `Appender`, `Level`, `Layout`, and `Filter` objects combined define a logging style. Another combination of these logging elements will result in a separate logging style. If we decide that all application components will collectively subscribe to a particular logging style, and when they switch over to a different logging style they do so collectively, then storing the configuration information in a database in a relational way might be the solution. This means each application component does not need to maintain and load its own configuration information, and we can control the logging behavior by changing the configuration information centrally in a database.

It is great that we can change logging behavior so easily, but how often do we need to do that? In general, we know before we write and deploy the application what information we will need to log to maintain it. We almost always need more logging information during the development and testing phase than we do in the deployment phase. The power of log4j lies not in the fact that we can change our application logging behavior every now and then, but in the fact that we can camouflage the capability to produce various degrees of logging information within an application, unveiling it when required. Only when we need more or less information do we switch over to a different style of logging.

The Database Table Design for Storing Logging Information

Recall that the structure of the properties-style configuration files and XML-style configuration files we used throughout the discussion of log4j is key value–based. To configure log4j from a database requires replicating the same information structure in the database. In a real-life situation, it could take a whole afternoon to decide what database structure to adopt. But for the sake of this example, we are going to use a pretty simplistic structure with two tables, LOGGER_REPOSITORY and APPENDER_DEF, that contain information about loggers and appenders, respectively.

Figure 6-2 shows the simple schema diagram for the tables we are going to use for this example.

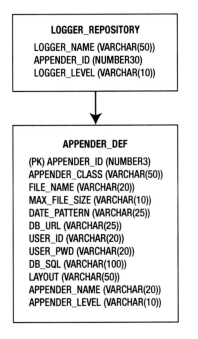

Figure 6-2. *The log4j configuration schema diagram*

This structure is a very simple one that excludes elements such as Filter objects and Renderer objects. We can see that the APPENDER_DEF table contains the possible properties related to different Appender objects, although to keep this example simple it does not include all the Appender objects. The database design in this example supports three appender objects: ConsoleAppender, DailyRollingFileAppender, and JDBCAppender.

The "Creating Configuration Data in the Database" section later in this chapter contains an example of configuration data in the tables.

Reading Configuration Information from the Database via the Configuration Loader

Once we have the configuration information defined in the database tables, we need some mechanism to read the information. We will now develop a small program that reads the configuration data from the database. It also creates a `java.util.Properties` object with the key and value of all the log4j configuration information and returns it to the caller. Once the data is read and loaded into the `Properties` object, the connection to the database is closed.

You might be wondering why we need to load the data in a `Properties` object. The reason will be clear once we go through this example. For the time being, you just need to know that we want to use the existing `org.apache.log4j.PropertyConfigurator` class to do the actual configuration job. The `PropertyConfigurator` class is capable of configuring the log4j framework from a `Properties` object.

Notice that the SQL statement to retrieve configuration data from the database is hard-coded within the `DBConfigLoader` class. We also retrieve the data by referencing the column names in the tables. All this is done to keep the example simple; feel free to improve this program by changing the infrastructure wherever you like.

Listing 6-5, `DBConfigLoader.java`, is a sample implementation for reading configuration information from the database.

Listing 6-5. *DBConfigLoader.java*

```java
package com.apress.logging.log4j;

import java.util.Properties;
import java.sql.Connection;
import java.sql.DriverManager;
import java.sql.Statement;
import java.sql.ResultSet;
import java.sql.SQLException;

public class DBConfigLoader
{
    private Connection conn = null;
    private String dbUrl = null;
    private String dbDriver = null;
    private String dbUser = null;
    private String dbPwd = null;

    /**
     * Constructor initializing the db access params
     */
    public DBConfigLoader()
    {
        this.setDbDriver("sun.jdbc.odbc.JdbcOdbcDriver");
        this.setDbUrl("jdbc:odbc:dbdef");
        this.setDbUser("system");
        this.setDbPwd("manager");
    }

    /**
     * Sets the driver class for the db access
     */
```

```java
    private void setDriver()
    {
        try
        {
            //load the driver
            Class.forName(dbDriver);
        } catch (ClassNotFoundException cnfe)
        {
            System.out.println("Could not find the driver class " +
dbDriver);
        }
    }

    /**
     * Method to obtain a db connection
     * @return Connection object
     * @throws SQLException
     */
    private Connection getConnection() throws SQLException
    {
        System.out.println("CONNECTION PARAMS: ");
        System.out.println("DRIVER: " + dbDriver);
        System.out.println("URL: " + dbUrl);
        System.out.println("USER: " + dbUser);
        System.out.println("PWD: " + dbPwd);
        //load the driver
        setDriver();
        //getting the connection
        conn = DriverManager.getConnection(dbUrl, dbUser, dbPwd);

        return conn;

    }

    /**
     * Obtain the configuration data from the db
     * @param sql The sql to execute to get the data
     * @return ResultSet object containing the data
     * @throws SQLException
     */
    private ResultSet getConfigData(String sql) throws SQLException
    {
        //obtain a connection to the database
        conn = getConnection();
        //create a statement object to execute the query
        Statement stmt = conn.createStatement();
        //execute the query to get the resultset
```

```java
        ResultSet rs = stmt.executeQuery(sql);
        return rs;
    }

    /**
     * constructs the SQL statement to execute
     * @return String the SQL statement
     */
    private String getSQL()
    {
        StringBuffer buffer = new StringBuffer("SELECT * FROM APPENDER_DEF
AD, LOGGER_REPOSITORY LR WHERE ");
        //buffer.append(" LR.LOGGER_NAME='" + loggerName + "' ");
        buffer.append(" LR.APPENDER_ID=AD.APPENDER_ID");
        System.out.println("The SQL: " + buffer.toString());
        return buffer.toString();
    }

    /**
     * Loads all the configuration data in a Properties object
     * and returns the Properties object back to the caller
     */
    public Properties getConfigData()
    {
        //properties object to store the config data
        Properties props = new Properties();
        String loggerName = null;
        String loggerLevel = null;
        String appenderName = null;
        String appenderClass = null;
        String appenderLevel = null;
        String fileName = null;
        String maxFileSize = null;
        String jdbcURL = null;
        String jdbcUser = null;
        String jdbcPwd = null;
        String jdbcSQL = null;
        String layout = null;

        //get the sql to obtain the config data
        String sql = getSQL();
        try
        {
            //get the result set
            ResultSet rs = getConfigData(sql);
            while (rs.next())
            {
```

```
              //getting the appender class
              appenderClass = rs.getString("APPENDER_CLASS");
              //getting the file name properties (can be null)
              fileName = rs.getString("FILE_NAME");
              //getting the max file size (can be null)
              maxFileSize = rs.getString("MAX_FILE_SIZE");
              //getting the jdbc url   (can be null)
              jdbcURL = rs.getString("DB_URL");
              //getting the jdbc user id (can be null)
              jdbcUser = rs.getString("USER_ID");
              //getting the jdbc password (can be null)
              jdbcPwd = rs.getString("USER_PWD");
              //getting the SQL string
              jdbcSQL = rs.getString("DB_SQL");
              //getting the layout information
              layout = rs.getString("LAYOUT");
              //getting the appender name
              appenderName = rs.getString("APPENDER_NAME");
              //getting the level of the appender
              appenderLevel = rs.getString("APPENDER_LEVEL");

              //getting the logger name
              loggerName = rs.getString("LOGGER_NAME");
              //getting the logger level
              loggerLevel = rs.getString("LOGGER_LEVEL");

              //constructing the properties with key and value
              String loggerKey = "log4j.logger." + loggerName;
              String appenderKey = "log4j.appender." + appenderName;

              //properties for the logger  level and the appender
              props.put(loggerKey, loggerLevel + "," + appenderName);
              props.put(getKey(appenderKey, null), appenderClass);

              if (fileName != null)
              {
                  props.put(getKey(appenderKey, "File"), fileName);
              }
              if (maxFileSize != null)
              {
                  props.put(getKey(appenderKey, "MaxFileSize"),
maxFileSize);
              }
              if (jdbcURL != null)
              {
                  props.put(getKey(appenderKey, "URL"), jdbcURL);
              }
```

```java
                    if (jdbcUser != null)
                    {
                        props.put(getKey(appenderKey, "user"), jdbcUser);
                    }
                    if (jdbcPwd != null)
                    {
                        props.put(getKey(appenderKey, "password"), jdbcPwd);
                    }
                    if (layout != null)
                    {
                        props.put(getKey(appenderKey, "layout"), layout);
                    }
                }
        } catch (SQLException sqle)
        {
            System.out.println("FAILED TO GET CONFIG DATA: " +
sqle.toString());
            sqle.printStackTrace();

        } finally
        {
            closeConnection();
        }

        return props;
    }


    /**
     * constructs the key for the properties object
     * @param prefix the prefix to the key
     * @param suffix  the suffix to the key
     * @return
     */
    private String getKey(String prefix, String suffix)
    {
        StringBuffer buffer = new StringBuffer(prefix);

        if (suffix != null)
        {
            buffer.append(".");
            buffer.append(suffix);
        }
        //System.out.println("returning key....."+buffer.toString());
        return buffer.toString();
    }
```

```java
private void closeConnection()
{
    try
    {
        if (conn != null)
        {
            conn.close();
        }
    } catch (SQLException sqle)
    {
        System.out.println("Problem closing the connection..");
    }
}

/**
 * Returns the db user name
 * @return   db user
 */

public String getDbUser()
{
    return dbUser;
}

/**
 * Sets the db user name
 * @param dbUser db user name
 */
public void setDbUser(String dbUser)
{
    this.dbUser = dbUser;
}

/**
 * Returns the database access password
 * @return the database password
 */
public String getDbPwd()
{
    return dbPwd;
}

/**
 * Sets the db access password
 * @param dbPwd   the db password
 */
public void setDbPwd(String dbPwd)
```

```
        {
            this.dbPwd = dbPwd;
        }

        /**
         * Returns the db driver
         * @return the db driver
         */
        public String getDbDriver()
        {
            return dbDriver;
        }

        /**
         * Sets the db driver
         * @param dbDriver the db driver
         */
        public void setDbDriver(String dbDriver)
        {
            this.dbDriver = dbDriver;
        }

        /**
         * Returns the db address
         * @return    the db address
         */
        public String getDbUrl()
        {
            return dbUrl;
        }

        /**
         * Sets the database address
         * @param dbUrl  the database address
         */
        public void setDbUrl(String dbUrl)
        {
            this.dbUrl = dbUrl;
        }
}
```

Writing the Configuration Class

Once we have loaded log4j configuration information from the database, we need some way to
access that information and configure log4j. To do this, we must write a custom configuration
class to read the data from the database and configure the log4j framework. The log4j API
already provides two classes for configuration: BasicConfigurator, which is capable of providing very basic configuration to the log4j framework, and DOMConfigurator, which is capable of

loading configuration information from an XML file. We can write our own configuration class to configure the log4j framework from a database. Before we do that, let's see how the configuration takes place within the log4j framework.

Figure 6-3 shows the sequence of the log4j initialization. Each time we try to obtain a Logger by calling Logger.getLogger(loggerName), the LogManager class gets initialized. LogManager collects and inspects the system properties supplied to log4j from the command line. Remember, this is happening at the class-loading time of the LogManager in a static block, and this takes place once and only once. LogManager detects the configuration files specified via the command line system properties. It then calls the OptionConverter helper class to parse the information contained in the files. The OptionConverter class instantiates an appropriate Configurator class and calls the doConfigure() method to complete the configuration process.

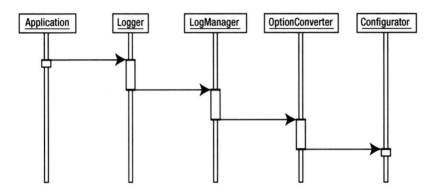

Figure 6-3. *The log4j configuration process*

Log4j relies on the fact that configuration information should be specified in a configuration file accessible through a URL. If no configuration resource file is specified, log4j tries to look for its default configuration file, log4j.properties, in the classpath of your application.

▓**Note** Starting with version 1.2.7, log4j looks for a log4j.xml or log4j.properties file in the classpath.

In case it cannot locate any configuration file, log4j exits, and application logging will no longer work. It is possible to override the configuration procedure by writing a custom configuration class that reads the configuration file from a location over the network. But this is restricted to only the protocols supported by the java.net.URL object.

Any custom configuration class we write must implement an interface named Configurator in log4j. The Configurator interface defines a single method, doConfigure(URL, LoggerRepository), which is the method in which the configuration takes place.

We have already seen that the log4j framework uses URL-based configuration. In our example, we wish to configure log4j by reading the configuration information from a database. There is a conflict of interest here because we are trying to do something that log4j does not support directly. But we will be clever by exploiting the existing framework to do our job. We will use a configuration file that contains information related to obtaining a connection to the database.

DBConfigurator will parse this configuration file and use the DBConfigLoader class to read the configuration information from the database. It will then obtain the java.util.Properties object from DBConfigLoader, which contains all the configuration information. The DBConfigurator class then uses the org.apache.log4j.PropertyConfigurator class to actually configure log4j by passing it the Properties object.

Listing 6-6, DBConfigurator.java, shows the custom configuration class we will use to configure the log4j framework.

Listing 6-6. *DBConfigurator.java*

```java
package com.apress.logging.log4j;

import org.apache.log4j.spi.Configurator;
import org.apache.log4j.spi.LoggerRepository;
import org.apache.log4j.PropertyConfigurator;
import org.apache.log4j.helpers.LogLog;

import java.net.URL;
import java.util.Properties;

public class DBConfigurator implements Configurator
{
    private String dbURL = null;
    private String dbUser = null;
    private String dbPwd = null;
    private String dbDriver = null;
    private DBConfigLoader configLoader = null;
    private Properties log4jProps = null;

    public DBConfigurator()
    {
        configLoader = new DBConfigLoader();
    }

    public void doConfigure(URL url, LoggerRepository repos)
    {
        Properties props = new Properties();
        try
        {
        //collect the db access information from the config file
        props.load(url.openStream());
        dbURL = (String)props.get("DB_URL");
        dbUser = (String)props.get("DB_USER");
        dbPwd = (String)props.get("DB_PWD");
        dbDriver = (String)props.get("DB_DRIVER");

        //configure the config loader
        configLoader.setDbDriver(dbDriver);
```

```
        configLoader.setDbUrl(dbURL);
        configLoader.setDbUser(dbUser);
        configLoader.setDbPwd(dbPwd);

        //get the log4j properties
        log4jProps = configLoader.getConfigData();
        //use the PropertyConfigurator to configure
        PropertyConfigurator.configure(log4jProps);
        }catch(Exception e)
        {
            LogLog.error("could not load the configuration ", e);
        }


    }
}
```

DBConfigurator implements the interface Configurator. Once the configuration class is specified as DBConfigurator, the LogManager class will pass the name of the configuration class to OptionConverter. OptionConverter will then create a new instance of DBConfigurator and call the doConfigure() method in it. Once the control is within the DBConfigurator class, DBConfigurator uses DBConfigLoader to obtain the configuration data and then uses PropertyConfigurator to do the actual log4j configuration.

In theory, we could configure log4j by calling PropertyConfigurator from within the DBConfigLoader class itself. But this means in the application we have to explicitly instantiate and call the configuration method of DBConfigLoader to do the configuration, which is not the ideal situation. If ever you need to use a different configuration class, you will have to change the source of your application to do so. Implementing the DBConfigurator class solves the problem and integrates the use of DBConfigLoader into the log4j framework. You might argue that DBConfigLoader is hard-coded within the DBConfigurator class, but we can easily extend DBConfigurator to read a system parameter indicating the database access class it should use, or we can specify the parameter within the configuration file.

A Database-Based Configuration Example

We now have the infrastructure ready to configure log4j from a database. Let's take a look at a small demo program, LoggingDemo.java, described in Listing 6-7. The class simply has a method to write two different logging messages with levels ERROR and INFO.

Listing 6-7. *LoggingDemo.java*

```
package com.apress.logging.log4j;
import org.apache.log4j.Logger;

public class LoggingDemo
{
    private static Logger logger = Logger.getLogger("APPLICATION1");
    public LoggingDemo()
    {
    }
```

```
    public void doLogging()
    {
        logger.info("INFO MESSAGE...");
        logger.error("ERROR MESSAGE...");

    }

    public static void main(String args[])
    {
        LoggingDemo demo = new LoggingDemo();
        demo.doLogging();
    }
}
```

Creating Configuration Data in the Database

In this sample program, we are trying to use a Logger object named APPLICATION1. We need to create a style for this named logger in the database. The following SQL script will insert a record for the logger named APPLICATION1, and for the corresponding appender record:

```
INSERT INTO LOGGER_REPOSITORY VALUES ('APPLICATION1','1,'ERROR');
```

Now we will create some appender configuration data in the APPENDER_DEF table. The following script will insert data for the Appender object with the ID 1:

```
INSERT INTO APPENDER_DEF VALUES
(1,'org.apache.log4j.ConsoleAppender', 'org.apache.log4j. SimpleLayout',
'CONSOLE', 'DEBUG');
```

The logger named APPLICATION1 will now have a level of ERROR and will use the Appender defined with the APPENDER_ID of 1 in the APPENDER_DEF table. Referring to the data we put in the APPENDER_DEF table, the Appender with ID value 1 is a ConsoleAppender. So any logging information from this application will be printed to the console. We can switch the entry in the LOGGER_REPOSITORY table any time to point the Appender to ID 2, which will then write logging data to the database using the JDBCAppender object.

The Configuration File

We also need a configuration file defining the database access parameters. Listing 6-8, dbConfig. properties, is the configuration file for this example.

Listing 6-8. *dbConfig.properties*

```
DB_DRIVER=sun.jdbc.odbc.JdbcOdbcDriver
DB_URL=jdbc:odbc:dbdef
DB_USER=system
DB_PWD=manager
```

Executing the Database-Based Configuration Program

Now we need to execute the program LoggingDemo with all the required system parameters passed to it in the following manner:

```
java –Dlog4j.configuration=dbConfig.properties –
Dlog4j.configuratorClass=com.apress.logging.log4j.DBConfigurator
com.apress.logging.log4j.LoggingDemo
```

Notice that only the message with the level ERROR is printed to the console. Change the logger level in the table to INFO, and both messages will be printed.

Custom Logging Framework

In an application, we want to trace every method entry and exit at the code optimization stage. Also, we want the level for these sorts of messages to be something below even the DEBUG level of log4j, as we do not want these messages to be published anytime after finishing the code optimization phase. It is inappropriate to use the DEBUG level for these sorts of messages because of the likelihood that in the future the DEBUG level for messaging may need to be turned on to debug the application. In such cases, the messages related to method entry and exit are more likely to convolute the logging trace. Considering all these factors, we will introduce a new level, TRACE, to the sample application.

Creating a Custom Level Class

We will now examine how to write a custom Level class. Each level basically corresponds to a static final unique integer value. We need to assign a unique integer value to the custom TRACE level we want to create. Also, log4j is capable of delegating logging messages to the UNIX Syslog via SysLogAppender. Therefore, each logging level defined also needs to define a Syslog equivalent. The constant integer values used for Syslog are defined in the Syslog specification. For example, one sample syslog.h file from the UNIX implementation contains the following Syslog constants defined for different levels of logging:

```
#define LOG_EMERG 0 /* system is unusable */
#define LOG_ALERT 1 /* action must be taken immediately */
#define LOG_CRIT 2 /* critical conditions */
#define LOG_ERR 3 /* error conditions*/
#define LOG_WARNING 4 /* warning conditions */
#define LOG_NOTICE 5 /* normal but significant conditions */
#define LOG_INFO 6 /* informational */
#define LOG_DEBUG 7 /* debug level messages */
```

The TRACE level should correspond to the LOG_DEBUG level of the Syslog implementation, and the Syslog equivalent for this level should be 7. Finally, the CustomLevel class needs to provide methods to return the appropriate Level object and to create a TRACE level from a given int or String value.

Listing 6-9, CustomLevel.java, demonstrates how to implement a custom Level class.

Listing 6-9. *CustomLevel.java*

```java
package com.apress.logging.log4j;

import org.apache.log4j.Level;

public class CustomLevel extends Level {

  static public final int  TRACE_INT  = Level.DEBUG_INT - 1;
  private static String TRACE_STR = "TRACE";

  public static final CustomLevel TRACE = new CustomLevel(TRACE_INT,
TRACE_STR, 7);

  protected CustomLevel(int level, String strLevel, int syslogEquiv) {
    super(level, strLevel, syslogEquiv);
  }

  public static Level toLevel(String sArg) {
    return (Level) toLevel(sArg, CustomLevel.TRACE);
  }

  public static Level toLevel(String sArg, Level defaultValue) {

    if(sArg == null) {
      return defaultValue;
    }
    String stringVal = sArg.toUpperCase();

    if(stringVal.equals(TRACE_STR)) {
      return CustomLevel.TRACE;
    }
    return Level.toLevel(sArg, (Level) defaultValue);
  }

  public static Level toLevel(int i) {
    switch(i) {
    case TRACE_INT: return CustomLevel.TRACE;
    }
    return Level.toLevel(i);
  }
}
```

In this CustomLevel object, we define a new level, TRACE, with a unique integer value that is one less than the unique integer value associated with the DEBUG level to keep the priority of DEBUG below DEBUG. This indicates that the TRACE level should be used in places where the priority is lowest. In the Syslog context, we assign it the Syslog equivalent 7 to correspond to LOG_DEBUG in the Syslog implementation.

Creating a Custom Logger

Once we have defined the CustomLevel object representing the level TRACE, we need a custom Logger object to use this level. Logger objects, in essence, have two responsibilities: They produce logging messages by delegating the logging request to different Appender objects with appropriate levels, and they return the instance of a named Logger object to the caller application. In the examples provided throughout the discussion of log4j, we have used the package name to name loggers. In reality, the name of a logger can be anything to identify the logger producing logging traces in a predefined destination.

In sophisticated application scenarios, we might decide to create several custom Logger classes. Depending on the name of the logger specified, we will return the appropriate Logger object to the caller application. We might also think about using a Factory object to decide which Logger object to return. The deciding criterion for returning an instance of a Logger may be the name of the logger.

Listing 6-10, CustomLogger.java, represents a custom Logger object with a method to produce TRACE-level messages. It also uses a CustomLoggerFactory object to create and return an appropriate custom Logger object.

Listing 6-10. *CustomLogger.java*

```
package com.apress.logging.log4j;

import org.apache.log4j.Logger;
import com.apress.logging.log4j.CustomLevel;

public class CustomLogger extends Logger {
    private String FQCN = CustomLogger.class.getName()+".";
    private static CustomLoggerFactory factory = new CustomLoggerFactory();
    public CustomLogger(String name) {
        super(name);
    }

    public void trace(Object message) {
        //call the super log method with throwable instance as null
        super.log(FQCN, CustomLevel.TRACE, message, null);

    }
    public static Logger getLogger(String name) {
        return Logger.getLogger(name, factory);
    }
}
```

This example of CustomLogger introduces a new method to publish TRACE-level messages to the destination specified through any Appender object associated with this Logger.

Generating a Custom Logger Factory Object

Listing 6-11, CustomLoggerFactory.java, is the code for generating a custom logger Factory object. The advantage of having a Factory object is that we can control how the Logger objects are made available to the caller application. The CustomLoggerFactory class implements the interface LoggerFactory and provides an implementation of the method makeNewLoggerInstance(String name). The sample implementation shows a skeleton of how the Factory object can be used to return different types of Logger objects.

Listing 6-11. *CustomLoggerFactory.java*

```
package com.apress.logging.log4j;

import org.apache.log4j.spi.LoggerFactory;
import org.apache.log4j.Logger;

public class CustomLoggerFactory implements LoggerFactory {
    public Logger makeNewLoggerInstance(String name) {
        return new CustomLogger(name);
    }
}
```

CustomLoggerFactory returns a separate CustomLogger instance based on the name of the Logger objects passed to it. This is the simplest possible scenario.

Using Custom Logging Components

You will now see a small example that demonstrates the use of the custom level, logger, and Factory object we created in the previous sections. As usual, the application that uses the logging mechanism will obtain an instance of the CustomLogger class. The application can then produce messages with the custom level TRACE by using the trace() method provided within the CustomLogger class.

Listing 6-12, CustomLoggerDemo.java, demonstrates the use of the CustomLogger class. Notice that the getLogger(String) method of the CustomLogger class actually returns an instance of the Logger class. For this reason, within the application we need to cast the returned instance to CustomLogger.

Listing 6-12. *CustomLoggerDemo.java*

```
package com.apress.logging.log4j;

import org.apache.log4j.Logger;

public class CustomLoggerDemo {
    private static CustomLogger logger =
(CustomLogger)CustomLogger.getLogger(CustomLoggerDemo.class.getPackage()
.getName());

    /** Creates a new instance of CustomLoggerDemo */
    public CustomLoggerDemo()
    {
    }
```

```
    public void doLogging()
    {
        logger.trace("THIS IS A TRACE LEVEL MESSAGE...");
    }

    public static void main(String args[])
    {
        CustomLoggerDemo demo = new CustomLoggerDemo();
        demo.doLogging();
    }
}
```

The doLogging() method uses the obtained CustomLogger instance and produces a TRACE-level message by using the trace() method of the CustomLogger class.

All this is nice and simple. But we still need to address a few things regarding the configuration settings for using the custom level, logger, and Factory object. When log4j is initialized, the framework tends to use a DefaultCategoryFactory object to configure the loggers. This DefaultCategory object returns a named instance of the Logger class. In order to use the CustomLoggerFactory class, we need to specify in the configuration file the CustomLoggerFactory class as the Factory class to be used within the framework. In case the framework uses the DefaultCategoryFactory class, we will get a ClassCastException in the caller application while attempting to cast the obtained logger instance to CustomLogger.

Also, as we are using the custom level TRACE, the configuration demands that the implementation class for this level also be defined. The custom level should be defined in level#classname format. Otherwise, the framework will not be able to use any level outside the domain of normal log4j-defined levels.

Listing 6-13, customlogger.properties, is the configuration file for the example in Listing 6-12.

Listing 6-13. *customlogger.properties*

```
#configure log4j to use the CustomLoggerFactory as the factory object
log4j.loggerFactory=com.apress.logging.log4j.CustomLoggerFactory

#set the level to TRACE and appender to ConsoleAppender
log4j.logger.com.apress.logging.log4j=TRACE#com.apress.logging.log4j
.CustomLevel,CONSOLE

#define the appender
log4j.appender.CONSOLE=org.apache.log4j.ConsoleAppender
log4j.appender.CONSOLE.layout=org.apache.log4j.SimpleLayout
```

Listing 6-14 shows the equivalent XML-style configuration for this example.

Listing 6-14. *customlogger.xml*

```
<?xml version="1.0" encoding="UTF-8"?>
<!DOCTYPE log4j:configuration SYSTEM "log4j.dtd">

<log4j:configuration xmlns:log4j="http://jakarta.apache.org/log4j/">
```

```
<appender name="A1" class="org.apache.log4j.ConsoleAppender">

  <layout class="org.apache.log4j.PatternLayout">
    <param name="ConversionPattern" value="%t %-5p %c{2} - %m%n"/>
  </layout>

</appender>

<logger name="com.apress.logging.log4j">
  <level value="TRACE" class="com.apress.logging.log4j.CustomLevel"/>
  <appender-ref ref="A1"/>
</logger>

<categoryFactory class="com.apress.logging.log4j.CustomLoggerFactory"/>

</log4j:configuration>
```

Notice how the custom `Level` and custom `LoggerFactory` classes are configured.

You have seen that by creating new levels and `Logger` classes, we are able to customize the priority of our logging messages.

▓Caution The creators of log4j strongly discourage the use of custom logger and custom logger `Factory` objects because they might interfere with the initialization process. I am presenting an example of how to use a custom logger and `Factory` objects in case the restriction is lifted in the future.

A Simpler Approach to Using a Custom Level Class

In the previous section, you saw how to extend the existing `Logger` class to create your own custom `Logger` class. One of the main motivations in subclassing the `Logger` class was to introduce a new logging method using a custom level, `TRACE`. To use the extended `Logger` class, we needed to create and supply a custom `LoggerFactory` class to the log4j framework. No doubt this all seems a bit complicated to achieve such a simple thing as adding a new method to the existing `Logger` class.

A simpler approach is to write a wrapper class around the existing `Logger` class. The wrapper class can provide the logging methods that are planned for the new logging features. Listing 6-15, `LoggerWrapper.java`, is an example of how we can use the custom level `TRACE` without getting into the complexities of subclassing the `Logger` class.

Listing 6-15. *LoggerWrapper.java*

```java
package com.apress.logging.log4j;

import org.apache.log4j.Logger;
import org.apache.log4j.Level;
```

```java
public class LoggerWrapper
 {
    private final String name;
    private Logger log;

    protected LoggerWrapper(String name)
    {
        this.name = name;
        log = Logger.getLogger(name);
    }

    public String getName()
    {
        return name;
    }

    public boolean isTraceEnabled()
    {
        if(!log.isEnabledFor(CustomLevel.TRACE))
            return false;
        else
            return
CustomLevel.TRACE.isGreaterOrEqual(log.getEffectiveLevel());
    }

    public void trace(Object message)
    {
        log.log(CustomLevel.TRACE, message);
    }

    public void trace(Object message, Throwable t)
    {
        log.log(CustomLevel.TRACE, message, t);
    }

    public boolean isDebugEnabled()
    {
        Level p = Level.DEBUG;
        if(!log.isEnabledFor(p))
            return false;
        else
            return p.isGreaterOrEqual(log.getEffectiveLevel());
    }

    public void debug(Object message)
    {
        log.log(Level.DEBUG, message);
    }
```

```java
public void debug(Object message, Throwable t)
{
    log.log(Level.DEBUG, message, t);
}

public boolean isInfoEnabled()
{
    Level p = Level.INFO;
    if(!log.isEnabledFor(p))
        return false;
    else
        return p.isGreaterOrEqual(log.getEffectiveLevel());
}

public void info(Object message)
{
    log.log(Level.INFO, message);
}

public void info(Object message, Throwable t)
{
    log.log(Level.INFO, message, t);
}

public void warn(Object message)
{
    log.log(Level.WARN, message);
}

public void warn(Object message, Throwable t)
{
    log.log(Level.WARN, message, t);
}

public void error(Object message)
{
    log.log(Level.ERROR, message);
}

public void error(Object message, Throwable t)
{
    log.log(Level.ERROR, message, t);
}

public void fatal(Object message)
{
    log.log(Level.FATAL, message);
}
```

```java
    public void fatal(Object message, Throwable t)
    {
        log.log(Level.FATAL, message, t);
    }

    public void log(Level p, Object message)
    {
        log.log(p, message);
    }

    public void log(Level p, Object message, Throwable t)
    {
        log.log(p, message, t);
    }

    public static LoggerWrapper getLogger(String name)
    {
        LoggerWrapper logger = new LoggerWrapper(name);
        return logger;
    }

    public static LoggerWrapper getLogger(Class clazz)
    {
        LoggerWrapper logger = new LoggerWrapper(clazz.getName());
        return logger;
    }
}
```

This implementation is pretty straightforward. It just uses an internal member of the org.apache.log4j.Logger class. It also mimics all the methods from the Logger class. Internally, it delegates the method calls to the instance of the Logger class. Notably, it provides a method to use the custom TRACE level and provides the method isTraceEnabled() to check if the level TRACE is enabled for any particular logger instance.

Listing 6-16, LoggerWrapperDemo.java, demonstrates a very simple use of the wrapper class we have just implemented.

Listing 6-16. *LoggerWrapperDemo.java*

```java
package com.apress.logging.log4j;

public class LoggerWrapperDemo
 {
    private static LoggerWrapper logger =
LoggerWrapper.getLogger(LoggerWrapperDemo.class.getPackage().getName());
    public LoggerWrapperDemo()
    {
```

```
    }
    public void doLogging(String message)
    {
        logger.trace(message);
    }

    public static void main(String args[])
    {
        LoggerWrapperDemo demo = new LoggerWrapperDemo();
        demo.doLogging("USING LOGGER WRAPPER TO DISPLAY TRACE LEVEL
MESSAGE");

    }
}
```

To execute this sample program, we need almost the same configuration file described in Listing 6-13, except that there is no logger Factory to be used for this example. The modified configuration file should read like the one in Listing 6-17, loggerWrapper.properties.

Listing 6-17. *loggerWrapper.properties*

```
#set the level to TRACE and appender to ConsoleAppender
log4j.logger.com.apress.logging.log4j=
TRACE#com.apress.logging.log4j.CustomLevel,CONSOLE

#define the appender
log4j.appender.CONSOLE=org.apache.log4j.ConsoleAppender
log4j.appender.CONSOLE.layout=org.apache.log4j.SimpleLayout
```

Executing the example program in Listing 6-16 with this configuration file will print the following TRACE-level message to the console:

```
TRACE - USING LOGGER WRAPPER TO DISPLAY TRACE LEVEL MESSAGE
```

By writing a simple wrapper class for the logger, we have avoided the complexities of writing custom Logger and custom LoggerFactory classes. This can be quite a useful technique for adding custom features to a custom Logger class while retaining the normal features of the default Logger class.

Writing a Custom Layout

The readability of logging information is vital to the success of any logging framework. Log4j offers tremendous flexibility in terms of how one wants to see the logging information. You might recall from Chapter 4 how PatternLayout offers a wide range of layout options.

However, we might want to create our own specific layout, it is possible to write any custom Layout object to plug in to the log4j framework. Listing 6-18 represents a custom layout example that will indent the logging messages based on the method name(s). Logging messages from the same method will get indented. This will increase the readability of the logging information. This layout will be something like the following:

```
DEBUG-main-initialised..

---INFO-main-obtained the connection..

------INFO-main-executed query..

---------INFO-main-parsed resultset..

------------INFO-main-populated objects..

--------------DEBUG-main-released resources..

DEBUG-doSomething-Inside do something method..
```

In the preceding example, logging messages from each method are indented by an indent character. Upon completion, the indentation is removed and started fresh for the next method.

Listing 6-18. *CustomLayout.java*

```java
package com.apress.logging.log4j;

import org.apache.log4j.Layout;

import org.apache.log4j.spi.LoggingEvent;

public class CustomLayout extends Layout{


    private String indenter = "---";

    private String separator = "-";

    private static int indentCounter = 0;

    private static String lastMethodName = null;


public String format(LoggingEvent event) {


        String currentMethodName = null;

        StringBuffer buffer = new StringBuffer();
```

```java
        currentMethodName = event.getLocationInformation().getMethodName();


        //check if this method name is different or not

        if(currentMethodName.equalsIgnoreCase(lastMethodName)){

            //add the indent

            for(int i = 0; i<indentCounter+1;i++){

                buffer.append(indenter);

            }


            //set the indent counter

            indentCounter++;

        }else{

            //reset the indent counter

            indentCounter = 0;

        }

        //construct the message buffer

        buffer.append(event.getLevel());

        buffer.append(separator);

        buffer.append(event.getRenderedMessage());

        buffer.append("\n");


        //set the last method name

        lastMethodName = currentMethodName;
```

```
        return buffer.toString();

    }



public boolean ignoresThrowable() {

        return true;

    }



public void activateOptions() {

        // nothing to do



    }



}
```

The meat of the preceding example is in the `format()` method. You may decide to do a lot more with this custom layout. For example, you might want to make the indent character or the set of logging information configurable. At the moment, only the level, method name, and logging messages are printed. Making the information to be published configurable will add a lot more value.

Conclusion

In this chapter, we have examined how to extend the existing log4j framework to write our own application-specific logging components. The plug-and-play nature of log4j makes it easy to integrate custom components into the existing framework. The default capability of log4j is versatile and meets most of the routine requirements in logging activity. However, you might venture to extend the existing framework should you really need it. This chapter provides a guideline for implementing custom logging components to use with log4j.

The next chapter presents a complete log4j example using the concepts discussed so far.

CHAPTER 7

■■■

A Complete log4j Example

To reinforce the concepts we have discussed thus far, let's consider an application that deals with several customer orders. The application processes the orders and sends appropriate responses back to the customers. All the orders the system processes are logged and can be used for future reference. Let's also assume that the system requires flexibility in terms of logging so that it can decide to log only orders with product codes falling within a certain range. The application will typically pass to the logging framework the order information to be printed. From a design point of view, the application will need to keep the logging methods generic and will have configurable appenders, filters, layouts, etc.

The application will use certain Logger(s), each of which will have its own set of appenders, filters, and layouts. It will be possible to change logging behavior completely by switching the Logger being used or by changing the associated appenders, filters, and layouts. This design will offer more flexibility for and maintainability of the system. From the logging point of view, this system will need the following objects to be in place:

- CustomerOrder: This object will hold the basic information about the order each customer is placing.

- ProductFilter: This object is capable of filtering the logging information based on a predefined product code range.

- OrderRenderer: This object is capable of rendering the CustomerOrder object as a String representation.

Listing 7-1, CustomerOrder.java, represents the business object that holds the customer order information.

Listing 7-1. *CustomerOrder.java*

```
package com.apress.business;

public class CustomerOrder {

    /** Holds value of property productName. */
    private String productName;

    /** Holds value of property productCode. */
    private int productCode;
```

```java
/** Holds value of property productPrice. */
private int productPrice;

/** Creates a new instance of CustomerOrder */
public CustomerOrder() {
}

public CustomerOrder(String name, int code, int price)
{
    this.productCode = code;
    this.productPrice = price;
    this.productName = name;
}


/** Getter for property productName.
 * @return Value of property productName.
 */
public String getProductName() {
    return this.productName;
}

/** Setter for property productName.
 * @param productName New value of property productName.
 */
public void setProductName(String productName) {
    this.productName = productName;
}

/** Getter for property productCode.
 * @return Value of property productCode.
 */
public int getProductCode() {
    return this.productCode;
}

/** Setter for property productCode.
 * @param productCode New value of property productCode.
 */
public void setProductCode(int productCode) {
    this.productCode = productCode;
}

/** Getter for property productPrice.
 * @return Value of property productPrice.
 */
```

```
    public int getProductPrice() {
        return this.productPrice;
    }

    /** Setter for property productPrice.
     * @param productPrice New value of property productPrice.
     */
    public void setProductPrice(int productPrice) {
        this.productPrice = productPrice;
    }
}
```

The program in Listing 7-2, ProductFilter.java, demonstrates the custom Filter object.
The ProductFilter object overrides the decide(LoggingEvent event) method from the Filter
class and inspects the product code of the CustomerOrder. If the product code is greater than 100,
ProductFilter accepts the logging request or else denies it. If the object passed to ProductFilter
is not an instance of the CustomerOrder, it remains neutral and allows the framework to invoke
the next filter in the chain.

Listing 7-2. *ProductFilter.java*

```
package com.apress.logging.log4j.filter;

import org.apache.log4j.spi.Filter;
import org.apache.log4j.spi.LoggingEvent;
import com.apress.business.CustomerOrder;

public class ProductFilter extends Filter
{

    /** Creates a new instance of ProductFilter */
    public ProductFilter() {
    }

    public int decide(LoggingEvent event)
    {
        int result=this.ACCEPT;
        //obtaining the message object passed through Logger
        Object message = event.getMessage();
        //checking if the message object is of correct type
        if(message instanceof CustomerOrder)
        {
            CustomerOrder order = (CustomerOrder)message;
            int productCode = order.getProductCode();
            //checking for the product code greater than 100 only
            if(productCode<100)
```

```
        {
            result = this.DENY;
        }
    }else
    {
        //this filter can ignore this, pass to next filter
        result = this.NEUTRAL;
    }

    return result;
    }
}
```

Once the ProductFilter approves the logging request, the logging event is passed to the associated Appender object. The Appender object will then pass the event to the associated Layout object, which then tries to render the logging message object into a String representation before formatting it according to any conversion pattern. In order for the Layout objects to successfully render the message, we need to have an ObjectRenderer for the CustomerOrder object. The program in Listing 7-3, OrderRenderer.java, implements the ObjectRenderer interface and provides an implementation of the doRender(Object obj) method. To keep the example simple, it returns a hyphen-separated list of the attribute values of the CustomerOrder object.

Listing 7-3. *OrderRenderer.java*

```
package com.apress.logging.log4j.renderer;

import org.apache.log4j.or.ObjectRenderer;
import com.apress.business.CustomerOrder;

public class OrderRenderer implements ObjectRenderer
{
    private static final String separator = "-";

    /** Creates a new instance of OrderRenderer */
    public OrderRenderer() {
    }

    public String doRender(Object obj)
    {
        StringBuffer buffer = new StringBuffer(50);
        CustomerOrder order = null;
        String productName = null;
        int productCode = 0;
        int productPrice = 0;
        //check if the instance is of correct type CustomerOrder
        if(obj instanceof CustomerOrder)
```

```
        {
            order = (CustomerOrder)obj;
            productName = order.getProductName();
            productCode = order.getProductCode();
            productPrice = order.getProductPrice();

            buffer.append(productName);
            buffer.append(separator);
            buffer.append(new Integer(productCode).toString());
            buffer.append(separator);
            buffer.append(new Integer(productPrice).toString());
        }

        return buffer.toString();
    }
}
```

Once we have all the objects ready, we need to pass the object hierarchy to the log4j framework. As discussed earlier, the ObjectRenderer can be configured only through DOMConfigurator, and we will define the logger configuration through an XML-style configuration file. Listing 7-4 shows the configuration file used for this example, filter_properties.xml.

Listing 7-4. *filter_properties.xml*

```
<?xml version="1.0" encoding="UTF-8"?>
<!DOCTYPE log4j:configuration SYSTEM "log4j.dtd">

<log4j:configuration xmlns:log4j="http://jakarta.apache.org/log4j/">

 <renderer renderedClass="com.apress.business.CustomerOrder"
renderingClass="com.apress.logging.log4j.renderer.OrderRenderer">
 </renderer>

 <appender name="A1" class="org.apache.log4j.ConsoleAppender">

   <layout class="org.apache.log4j.PatternLayout">
     <param name="ConversionPattern" value="%t %-5p %c{2} - %m%n"/>
   </layout>
   <filter class="com.apress.logging.log4j.filter.ProductFilter"/>
 </appender>

 <logger name="com.apress.logging.log4j">
   <level value="debug"/>
   <appender-ref ref="A1"/>
 </logger>
</log4j:configuration>
```

Finally, Listing 7-5 presents a sample application to demonstrate the filtering of the log messages and rendering of the CustomerOrder object.

Listing 7-5. *ProductFilterDemo.java*

```java
package com.apress.logging.log4j;

import org.apache.log4j.Logger;
import com.apress.business.CustomerOrder;
import com.apress.logging.log4j.filter.ProductFilter;
import com.apress.logging.log4j.renderer.OrderRenderer;
public class ProductFilterDemo
{
    private static Logger logger =
Logger.getLogger(ProductFilterDemo.class.getPackage().getName());

    /** Creates a new instance of ProductFilterDemo */
    public ProductFilterDemo() {
    }

    public void processOrder(CustomerOrder order)
    {
        logger.info(order);
    }

    public static void main(String args[])
    {
        CustomerOrder order1 = new CustomerOrder("Beer", 101, 20);
        CustomerOrder order2 = new CustomerOrder("Lemonade", 95, 10);
        CustomerOrder order3 = new CustomerOrder("Chocolate", 223, 5);

        ProductFilterDemo demo = new ProductFilterDemo();
        demo.processOrder(order1);
        demo.processOrder(order2);
        demo.processOrder(order3);
    }

}
```

This application creates three different CustomerOrder objects with different product names, product codes, and product prices. The processOrder() method simply logs the CustomerOrder object passed to it. With the ProductFilter object in place, executing the application in Listing 7-5 will result in the following log messages being printed, excluding any having product codes below 100:

```
main INFO  logging.log4j - Beer-101-20
main INFO  logging.log4j - Chocolate-223-5
```

Conclusion

This chapter demonstrates the use of several log4j components in a real-life scenario. The configuration file used for these examples is in XML style because the `Filter` object and `Renderer` object can be configured only via XML style. This chapter also illustrates the simplicity and great extendibility of log4j. With simple components plugged in to the framework, log4j can achieve so much powerful logging. In the next chapter, we will examine how log4j fits into the J2EE world.

Log4j and J2EE

With the coming of J2EE and J2EE-enabled containers, life has become simpler. Programmers can concentrate on programming the business and application logic, without wasting much time on low-level issues such as threading, concurrency, transaction, etc. On the other hand, life has also become more complex as the J2EE containers and application servers behave like a closed system and the basic J2EE container infrastructure works like black magic. It is important to understand how to package the log4j components in the context of a J2EE application.

In this chapter, I will discuss the issues surrounding the use of log4j with J2EE applications and try to provide solutions to those problems.

Why Logging Is Difficult in J2EE

Logging in J2EE applications is complex because of several contributing factors. Moreover, the logging requirements can vary depending on the type of application. For example, in a simple J2EE-based Web application, it might be sufficient just to log the access and operations performed, but in a complex application, you might need to log information about users accessing the application, time of access, and the sequence of operations performed by a particular user.

In general, you should note the following characteristics of logging in the J2EE environment:

- *Distributed*: J2EE is distributed by nature. Any logging activity associated with the J2EE environment must also be distributed.

- *Multi-User*: Multiple users from various locations often access J2EE applications.

- *Clustered*: J2EE applications are often deployed in a clustered environment to enhance performance. Maintaining log information across multiple clusters is a challenge.

- *Centralized*: Logging information needs to be centralized to be effective.

- *Chronological*: In many J2EE applications, order of information is very important. We need to ensure that logging information is in chronological order.

- *Identification*: Logging information needs to be stamped with some unique identifier to separate one invoker from another. Otherwise, information is too large to filter against any particular operation or user, or against the invoker of the application.

Despite these issues, log4j does work in J2EE containers. The only time it does not work is when the log4j elements are not correctly placed in an appropriate classpath. The J2EE containers apply multiple and customized class loaders to load and deploy various components of a J2EE application. Depending upon where the log4j-specific components are bundled, specific class loaders have access to those components, and access to different parts of the J2EE application is allowed or restricted.

Thus, in order to correctly deploy log4j-enabled applications, you need to understand how the application server applies the class loaders to load specific components of a J2EE application. In the following section, I will discuss the class-loading issues with WebLogic 8.1 and explain the use of log4j with the WebLogic application server.

WebLogic Class Loaders Explained

The WebLogic application server uses its custom class loaders on top of the native class loader supplied by the JVM. Any J2EE application within WebLogic is bundled and deployed as a .ear file. An application's .ear file consists of

- One or more Enterprise Java Beans (EJB) .jar files.

- One or more Web-application .war files.

- A Resource Adapter .rar file containing the specific extension used for database access, etc.

There are two ways you can deploy applications into WebLogic:

- Deploy the EJB and the Web application separately. This way, different class loaders load the EJB and the Web application. Because the class loaders are different, components are specific to each application boundary and not visible to each other.

- Package both the EJB and Web application in a .ear file and deploy it as a single application. This way, the whole application gets its own class loader hierarchy. It is important to note that although a specific .ear file is loaded with one class loader, separate class loaders load individual Web applications. The EJBs are loaded with the root class loader (i.e., the application class loader).

░**Note** Application code has visibility only of classes loaded by the application's own class loader and its parent class loader.

Figure 8-1 explains the WebLogic class loader concepts.

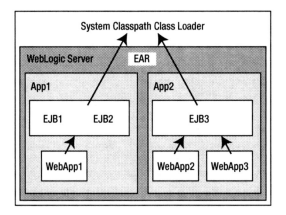

Figure 8-1. *WebLogic class loader concepts*

So what happens to resources shared between the EJBs and the Web application within a J2EE application? Do we need to bundle the EJB .jar file(s) and the Web application .war file(s) individually? In WebLogic, any .jar file shared between the EJB and the Web application must be placed in /APP-INF/lib and the shared class files must be placed in the /APP-INF/classes folder.

For example, in Figure 8-1, within the application App1, the file APP-INF/lib/XYZ.jar is available to EJB1, EJB2, and the WebApp1.

■**Note** This does not work the other way round; i.e., it is not possible to swap the .jar file and class files.

When Log4j Does Not Work

You now have a proper understanding of how WebLogic class loaders behave and how the resources are handled within WebLogic. We shall now create some scenarios in which log4j will not work properly for a J2EE application.

Case 1

If we use log4j in EJB1, EJB2, and WebApp1 in the example in Figure 8-1 and bundle the log4j.jar file within the WEB-INF/lib folder of WebApp1, log4j will not work correctly. In this scenario, as WebApp1 is loaded by a different class loader, EJB1 and EJB2 will not able to find the log4j.jar file and, hence, logging will fail for the EJBs. On the other hand, if you alter the position of the log4j.jar files and place them into the EJBs only, log4j will not work correctly. In this case, logging will fail for the Web application (WebApp1).

Case 2

If we put log4j.jar and the log4j configuration file at the root level of the WebLogic application server, the system class loader will load it (as in Figure 8-1). If both App1 and App2 use two Loggers with same name, the first Logger's configuration will be overridden by the Logger configuration of the application that was loaded later. So information from App1 might end up in the log file of App2.

■**Note** This is a problem only when more than one application is deployed within the same WebLogic domain.

Case 3

When App1 collaborates with App2 (as in Figure 8-1), two separate .ear files are involved. In this situation, we are cutting across class loaders. If you are using thread-specific identifiers to isolate callers of the application, then you are out of luck with log4j bundled within two separate .ear files; because we are cutting across class loaders, class loaders and thread information will not be passed from the caller to the called application.

Case 4

If a J2EE application is deployed in a clustered environment and you use FileAppender to log messages, a copy of the log file will be created in every cluster and information will be scattered. This means that tracing any important log message will be more difficult.

Making Log4j Work in J2EE

The key to making log4j work is simply to avoid the pitfalls discussed in the previous section. The right solution depends on the project and the environment. The following are few strategies that you might adopt:

■**Note** This discussion is based on a WebLogic application server. Similar principles will apply to other application servers. However, the exact naming of the folders might change.

- If you want to share the same log4j components across the EJB and Web applications, always package the EJB and Web application into a .ear file. Also, place the log4j-specific .jar files in /APP-INF/lib, and any log4j extended classes and the log4j configuration file within the /APP-INF/classes folder.

- If you want to use separate log4j configuration files for Web applications and the EJBs, you have to place the Web application's log4j configuration file in the /WEB-INF/classes folder, and the EJBs' configuration file in the individual .jar files. This way the Web application will have visibility of its own log4j configuration file through its own class loader, and the EJBs will get their log4j configuration file through their individual class loader.

- If you want to share the log4j components across all the applications deployed in a single domain, you may decide to put the log4j components in the system classpath. But be careful in naming the Loggers to avoid the Case 2 scenario mentioned in the previous section.

- If you are deploying a single J2EE application in a clustered environment, refrain from using FileAppender. Use SocketAppender, JMSAppender, etc. to centralize the logging information.

■**Note** According to EJB specifications, it is best to avoid using File I/O from EJBs. Hence, it is best not to use FileAppender directly from within EJBs.

- If order is important for logging, do not rely on JMS-based logging as JMS does not guarantee the order of messages in a clustered environment.

■**Note** Some argue that having a date and timestamp will solve the ordering problem with JMS-based logging. But unfortunately, this is not true as the JVM time is not unique. It works with a resolution of 10 milliseconds. JMS *can* guarantee order in a single-cluster environment, but *not* with multiple clusters.

Sometimes It Works on Its Own

Many application servers, such as WebLogic, use log4j for their internal logging. In this case, there is a default log4j configuration file in the system classpath. It is accessible to all the applications deployed within WebLogic. This default configuration file defines a root Logger, which also is available to all the applications.

In this context, if one application is using log4j to log messages but has not explicitly provided a log4j configuration file to use within that application context, there is no logger configuration to handle the logging calls from the application. In log4j, the onus of logging then falls on any root Logger specified. Hence, the root Logger configuration specified within the system-wide WebLogic's internal log4j configuration file takes over and you might still see some logging information being published magically. The key will be to notice that and make sure the application-specific log4j configuration file is provided.

Conclusion

This chapter focused on issues regarding the use of log4j in a J2EE environment. We have discussed the challenges of logging within a J2EE environment and demonstrated how log4j can be used within WebLogic by understanding the class-loading issues in WebLogic. Once you know how individual J2EE containers deal with different parts of a J2EE application, it will be fairly easy to figure out how to package log4j in your J2EE application.

Using the Apache Log Tag Library

One of the many advantages of a powerful logging framework such as Apache log4j is that it is not restricted to any particular application scenario. Apache log4j is a robust and extensible logging framework that can be tailored to any application-specific need. One feature that makes this logging framework so robust is the Log tag library, which is part of the Jakarta Taglibs project.

The Log tag library allows developers to embed log4j-based logging activity within a JavaServer Pages (JSP). In essence, it provides tags pertaining to all the logging levels declared by log4j and uses a configuration file to configure the log4j framework required to perform the logging activity.

In this chapter, we will examine the use of the Log tag library and see how we can extend it to incorporate our own logging tags.

What Is a Tag?

In Model 2 of Model-View-Controller (MVC) architecture, it is recommended to have a clear separation between the presentation of data and any sort of data-processing or data-computation logic. In the early days of JSP, developers used the Java scripting within JSP. This not only violated the concept of the MVC pattern, but also made JSP unreadable and difficult to maintain.

Nevertheless, developers do need to use presentation logic (business logic is a big no-no at the presentation layer) to present and format data. For example, iterating through a list of data and writing the data in a formatted way is a classic case for using Java scripts within JSP.

To conform to the Model 2 MVC pattern and achieve clear separation between presentation, data access, and data formatting logics, JSP tags were invented. You can create custom tags (similar to HTML or JSP tags) and embed any data-computing or data-formatting logics within the tag. The custom tag then can be used within a JavaServer Page. By using these custom tags, JavaServer Pages remain as pure view, meaning they contain only code related to formatting, and display specific items such as styles, and so on; all the computation and processing logics are delegated to the tags and are not visible to the JSP coder.

A collection of custom JSP tags can be placed within a tag library.

Installing the Log Tag Library

Installing and using Log with JSP is pretty straightforward. Follow these steps to set up and use Log in a Web application:

1. First, obtain the binary distribution of Log (1.1) from the Apache Web site
   (http://jakarta.apache.org/taglibs/doc/log-doc/intro.html).

2. Extract the archive file to any convenient location on the local machine.

3. Copy the tag library descriptor file, taglibs-log.tld, to the application-specific /WEB-INF subdirectory.

4. Copy the taglibs-log.jar file to the /WEB-INF/lib subdirectory of the Web application.

5. Add a <taglib> ELEMENT to the web.xml file of the Web application to specify the location of the tag library descriptor as shown here:

```
<taglib>
  <taglib-uri>http://jakarta.apache.org/taglibs/log-1.0</taglib-uri>
  <taglib-location>/WEB-INF/log.tld</taglib-location>
</taglib>
```

This is all we need to do to use Log in a Web application. Now you will see a simple example of using Log from within a JavaServer Page.

▦Note The installation procedure described in this section is specific to the Apache Tomcat Web server environment. For using Log (1.1) with other Web servers, you need to configure it to work specifically with the Web server you are using.

A Simple Example of Using the Log Tag Library

First, let's see a simple example of how we can use the Log tag library within a JSP to perform logging through log4j. Listing 9-1, SimpleLog.jsp, is a straightforward JSP that uses the Log tag library to print logging information to the console of a Web server. This example is demonstrated using Tomcat 3.2.1.

Listing 9-1. *SimpleLog.jsp*

```
<html>
<%@ taglib uri="http://jakarta.apache.org/taglibs/log-1.0" prefix="log" %>
<BODY>
<h1>Test Log Tag Library</h1>
<log:debug>Message embedded within open and close tags.</log:debug>
<log:debug message="Message passed as an attribute to the tag" />
<log:info category="test">Using category attribute.</log:info>
You should see output in the debug logs now.
</BODY>
</html>
```

As you can see, this JSP, although very simple, is enough to show how the Log tag libraries work. In this example, we are using the <debug> and <info> tags to print logging information. The Log tag library provides tags related to all the levels of logging defined in log4j. We will see all the tags available with Log later in this chapter. For the time being, let's explore the basics of using Log from within a JSP:

- First, we need to import the Log tag library into our JSP to make the tags available to the page context. The following line of code within the JSP achieves this:

```
<%@ taglib uri=http://jakarta.apache.org/taglibs/log-1.0
    prefix="log" %>
```

- This line of code imports the tag library from the specified location and sets log as the tag name prefix for the tags in the library. In reality, this prefix can be any unique text. The tags from the Log tag library need to begin with the prefix that is defined while importing the tag library to the page.

- The tags accept optional attributes and require open and close tags for each of them.

Now let's take a look at the configuration requirements for this example.

Configuration File for the Log Tag Library

The Log tag library uses log4j to print logging information to a desired location. As mentioned in Chapter 2, log4j does not make any assumptions about the application environment. To obtain logging information in a desired format and at a desired location, log4j needs a configuration file specifying all the information about the formatting and the destination of the logging information.

Log supplies a default configuration file named log4j.properties. Listing 9-2 describes the default log4j configuration file that is shipped with the Log distribution.

Listing 9-2. *log4j.properties, the Default Configuration File for Log*

```
# Sample properties to initialize log4j
log4j.rootCategory=debug, stdout

log4j.appender.stdout=org.apache.log4j.ConsoleAppender
log4j.appender.stdout.layout=org.apache.log4j.PatternLayout

# Pattern to output the caller's file name and line number.
log4j.appender.stdout.layout.ConversionPattern=%5p [%t] (%F:%L) - %m%n

log4j.appender.R=org.apache.log4j.RollingFileAppender
log4j.appender.R.File=logtags.log

log4j.appender.R.MaxFileSize=100KB
# Keep one backup file
log4j.appender.R.MaxBackupIndex=2

log4j.appender.R.layout=org.apache.log4j.PatternLayout
log4j.appender.R.layout.ConversionPattern=%p %t %c - %m%n
```

This configuration file is quite simple. It uses ConsoleAppender and RollingFileAppender objects to output logging information to a Web server console and to a file. It also uses PatternLayout to format the logging information. The pattern specified for the logging information to be printed to the console includes the level, thread name, filename, location information, and message followed by a newline character.

The pattern for writing to a file is slightly different and includes the level, thread name, logger name, and message followed by a newline character. Although this configuration file looks simple, it highlights the following important points as to how Log works:

- Log uses the log4j root logger (synonymous with Category in the preceding example) to publish the logging information. The root logger has the threshold level DEBUG.

- Log, by default, writes logging information to the Web server console. In theory, Log can be configured to send logging information to any preferred destination by changing the configuration file. It provides a sample configuration for redirecting logging information to a rolling file by using the RollingFileAppender object.

- If we want to use a logger other than the root logger, then we need to configure the Logger object in the configuration file. Forgetting to do that may result in no logging information printing to any of the specified destinations.

- Changing the threshold level for the root logger or other custom loggers used with any of the tags can cause changes in the logging output.

▓**Note** If no separate logger (Category) is explicitly specified as an attribute of any of the Log tags, then the tags rely on the root logger of log4j to publish logging information. Hence, it is always safe to keep the root logger configuration even though we may specify custom logger (Category) names within the tag attributes and configure them separately in the same configuration file.

Setting the Environment

Having followed the instructions in the "Installing the Log Tag Library" section, you are ready to use the Log tag library from within a JSP. Before we can see the example JSP in Listing 9-1 in action, we need to configure the Web server to use the JSP and the log4j configuration file as described in the next few steps:

1. First, put the JSP described in Listing 9-1 into a folder named TestLogTags (or any folder of your choice) under the webapps directory of the Tomcat installation.

2. In Tomcat, any Web application typically contains a WEB-INF directory and a WEB-INF/ classes directory. Place the log4j.properties file in one of these locations.

3. Go to the tomcat.bat file in %TOMCAT_HOME%\bin.

4. Add an entry to set the classpath variable to point to the directory containing the log4j.properties file. For this example, the entry may read as follows:

```
set CP=%CP%;C:\Jakarta-tomcat-3.2.1\webapps\
    TestLogTags\WEB-INF\classes
```

5. Add the following entry to the tomcat.bat file:

```
set TOMCAT_OPTS=-Dlog4j.configuration=log4j.properties
```

You might also recall that log4j, by default, looks for the `log4j.properties` or `log4j.xml` file in the classpath. If you place one of these files in the TOMCAT classpath (or under WEB-INF/classes in your application), you can skip step 5. However, if you name your configuration file in a different way, you will need to perform this step.

▓**Note** We can also configure log4j through an initialization servlet. Consult Chapter 2 for more on this topic.

The Log Example in Action

Now start up Tomcat and access the JSP page, as shown in Figure 9-1. Tomcat will load the `log4j.properties` file, and Log will use this configuration file to print the logging information.

Test Log (1.1) Tag Library

You should see output in the debug logs now.

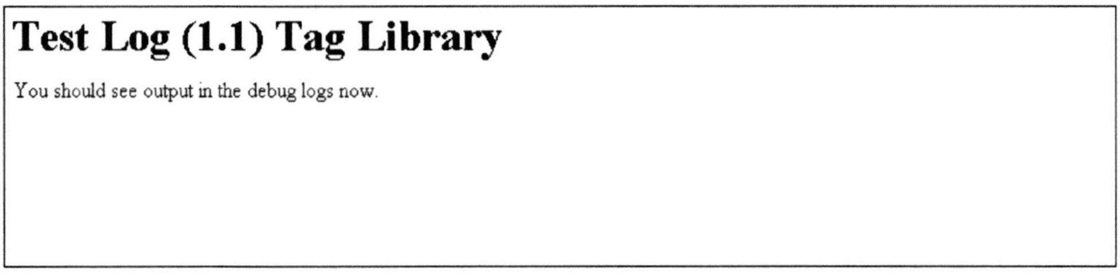

Figure 9-1. *The SimpleLog.jsp page*

If we now look at the Tomcat console, we will see the following logging information printed:

```
DEBUG [Thread-11] (LoggerTag.java:109) - Message embedded within open and
close tags.
DEBUG [Thread-11] (LoggerTag.java:97) - Message passed as an attribute to
the tag
 INFO [Thread-11] (LoggerTag.java:109) - Using category attribute.
```

Using a Custom Logger with the Log Tag Library

In the JSP in Listing 9-1, we use the `<log:info>` tag with the category attribute specified as test. This is the name of the logger to be produced as part of the logging information. If we change the output pattern for the logging information to include information about the logger, we will see the category test appearing as part of the logging output. The whole point of specifying the category attribute is to be able to include a different set of configuration parameters for the category or logger.

Listing 9-3 presents a modified `log4j.properties` file that includes configuration for the category named test.

Listing 9-3. *Modified log4j.properties File*

```
# Sample properties to initialize log4j
log4j.rootCategory=debug, stdout
log4j.logger.test=debug, R

log4j.appender.stdout=org.apache.log4j.ConsoleAppender
log4j.appender.stdout.layout=org.apache.log4j.PatternLayout

# Pattern to output the caller's file name and line number.
log4j.appender.stdout.layout.ConversionPattern=%5p [%t] (%F:%L) - %m%n

log4j.appender.R=org.apache.log4j.RollingFileAppender
log4j.appender.R.File=logtags.log

log4j.appender.R.MaxFileSize=100KB
# Keep one backup file
log4j.appender.R.MaxBackupIndex=2

log4j.appender.R.layout=org.apache.log4j.PatternLayout
log4j.appender.R.layout.ConversionPattern=%p %t %c - %m%n
```

This configuration file defines the configuration for the logger test. The test logger has a threshold level of DEBUG and uses a RollingFileAppender object to print logging information to a file named logtags.log. Notice that the conversionPattern to format the logging information includes the name of the logger (%c).

Using this configuration file for Log will write information to the logtags.log file in the %TOMCAT_HOME%\bin directory. If we execute the example JSP with this modified configuration file, we will see the following output in the logtags.log file:

```
DEBUG Thread-11 root - Message embedded within open and close <log> tags.
DEBUG Thread-11 root - Message passed as an attribute to the <log> tag
INFO Thread-11 test - Hello how are you?
```

This is how we can use different loggers with custom configuration to handle logging information. If we specify the category attribute in the JSP but do not specify a configuration for it, Log will use the root logger configuration to handle the logging request.

Description of Log Tags

The Log tag library provides tags corresponding to the levels declared in log4j. Table 9-1 summarizes all the Log tag library tags and their attributes.

Table 9-1. *Summary of Log Tags*

Tag Name	Tag Description	Attribute Name	Required
debug	Displays a DEBUG-level message	category	No
		message	No
info	Displays an INFO-level message	category	No
		message	No

Tag Name	Tag Description	Attribute Name	Required
warn	Displays a WARN-level message	category message	No No
error	Displays an ERROR-level message	category message	No No
fatal	Displays a FATAL-level message	category message	No No
dump	Displays all the variables in a specified scope	scope	Yes

As you can see, the use of these Log tags is very simple. All the tags except dump have two optional attributes, category and message. It is possible to specify the logging information as a value of the message attribute or by enclosing it within the tag. For example, we can use the error tag in the following two ways:

```
<log:error message="This is an error message"> </log:error>
<log:error>This is an error message</log:error>
```

The dump tag mentioned in Table 9-1 is designed to print all variables within the scope specified through the scope attribute. Listing 9-4, SimpleLogDump.jsp, is a modified version of the JSP in Listing 9-1 and adds a dump tag within the page.

Listing 9-4. *SimpleLogDump.jsp*

```
<html>
<%@ taglib uri="http://jakarta.apache.org/taglibs/log-1.0" prefix="log" %>
<BODY>
<h1>Test Log Tag Library</h1>
<log:debug>Message embedded within open and close tags.</log:debug>
<log:debug message="Message passed as an attribute to the tag" />
<log:info category="test">Using category attribute.</log:info>
You should see output in the debug logs now.
<H4>request</H4>
<log:dump scope="request" />
<H4>page</H4>
<log:dump scope="page" />
<H4>session</H4>
<log:dump scope="session" />
<H4>application</H4>
<log:dump scope="application" />
</BODY>
</html>
```

In this JSP, we are displaying the output of the dump tag with all the possible scope attribute values. Figure 9-2 shows what is displayed on the page.

Figure 9-2. *The SimpleLogDump.jsp page*

Creating Custom Tags with the Log Tag Library to Use a Custom Level

In Chapter 6, you saw how to write a custom Level class, TRACE, and use it with log4j. If we want to use the TRACE custom level along with the Log tag library, we have to extend the Log tag library framework. Typically, we can do so by performing the following tasks:

- Write a new Tag class to represent the custom level TRACE.

- Make the new Tag and Level classes available to the application.

- Modify the taglib-descriptor file to describe the new tag.

In the following sections of this chapter, we will examine how we can achieve these tasks to use the TRACE level with the Log tag library.

Creating a New Tag

In the Log tag library world, all tag classes are subclasses of the abstract class called LoggerTag. The LoggerTag class is a subclass of the BodyTagSupport class and does the entire job of handling tag-related operations. It also defines an abstract method, getPriority(), that is implemented in all other subclasses of the LoggerTag class. All other tag classes, such as ErrorTag, InfoTag, etc., are subclasses of LoggerTag and provide implementations for the getPriority() method. Thus, to define a new tag, we simply need to extend the LoggerTag class and provide an implementation of the getPriority() method that returns the custom level TRACE. Listing 9-5, TraceTag.java, demonstrates how to write a custom tag using the custom level TRACE.

Listing 9-5. *TraceTag.java*

```
package com.apress.logging.log4j.customtag;

import org.apache.taglibs.log.LoggerTag;
import org.apache.log4j.Priority;
import com.apress.logging.log4j.CustomLevel;

public class TraceTag extends LoggerTag
 {
    protected Priority getPriority()
    {
        return CustomLevel.TRACE;
    }
}
```

To develop this custom tag, we reuse the custom level TRACE developed in Chapter 6 (refer to Listing 6-9). As you can see, creating a new tag to use a new level is straightforward. Listing 9-6 shows the tag library description that needs to be added to the existing taglibs-log.tld file (which is shipped with the Log distribution).

Listing 9-6. *Tag Description for the Custom TraceTag*

```
<tag>
    <name>trace</name>
    <tagclass>com.apress.logging.log4j.customtag.TraceTag</tagclass>
    <attribute>
      <name>category</name>
      <required>false</required>
      <rtexprvalue>true</rtexprvalue>
    </attribute>
    <attribute>
      <name>message</name>
      <required>false</required>
      <rtexprvalue>true</rtexprvalue>
    </attribute>
  </tag>
```

Note The name of the tag is specified as trace. Therefore, within a JSP, we need to use the name trace to access this tag.

The Custom TraceTag in Action

Once we have the tag class for the level TRACE ready and we modify the taglibs-log.tld file to incorporate the definition of the new trace tag, we can start using it in a JSP. In order to set up Tomcat to use this new tag, we will need to perform the following steps:

1. Copy the required new TraceTag and CustomLevel class in the appropriate directory structure within the Web application. For example, if the Web application directory is TestLogTags, then the appropriate package structure for the classes will need to be created under the TestLogTags\WEB-INF\classes directory.

2. Edit the Tomcat.bat file to include the taglibs-log.jar file in the classpath.

3. Modify the log4j.properties file to set the threshold level to TRACE. The default threshold level set for the root logger is DEBUG, which is above the level of TRACE. So with default configuration, TRACE-level messages will not be published. Listing 9-7 presents the modified log4j.properties file for using the TRACE level.

Listing 9-7. *Modified log4j.properties File for Using the TRACE Level*

```
log4j.rootCategory=trace#com.apress.logging.log4j.CustomLevel, stdout

log4j.appender.stdout=org.apache.log4j.ConsoleAppender
log4j.appender.stdout.layout=org.apache.log4j.PatternLayout

# Pattern to output the caller's filename and line number.
log4j.appender.stdout.layout.ConversionPattern=%5p [%t] (%F:%L) - %m%n

log4j.appender.R=org.apache.log4j.RollingFileAppender
log4j.appender.R.File=logtags.log

log4j.appender.R.MaxFileSize=100KB
# Keep one backup file
log4j.appender.R.MaxBackupIndex=2

log4j.appender.R.layout=org.apache.log4j.PatternLayout
log4j.appender.R.layout.ConversionPattern=%p %t %c - %m%n
```

With these settings in place, execute the JSP presented in Listing 9-8. This JSP includes a TRACE-level message.

Listing 9-8. *SimpleLogTrace.jsp*

```
<html>
<%@ taglib uri="http://jakarta.apache.org/taglibs/log-1.0" prefix="log" %>
<BODY>
<h1>Test Log Tag Library</h1>
<log:trace>Trace level message.</log:trace>
You should see output in the debug logs now.
</BODY>
</html>
```

Executing this JSP will produce the following message with the TRACE level in the Web server console:

```
TRACE [Thread-11] (LoggerTag.java:109) - Trace level message.
```

Conclusion

In this chapter, we discussed a newly released tag library, Log, for using log4j within a JSP to perform logging. This solves the age-old problem of how to establish controlled logging from within a JSP. By changing the configuration, it is possible to redirect logging information to any preferred destination in any desired format. But careful consideration is required before you include in your Web application CPU-intensive logging operations such as writing logging data to a database, as it might affect the performance of that application.

This brings us to the end of the log4j discussion. All the topics explained in Chapters 2 through 9 should help you understand the internals of log4j and how to use it in practical applications. The smaller examples in these chapters should enable you to grasp the concepts presented and see quick results to better understand the use of log4j. The more extensive examples should help you correlate the use of log4j with real-life applications.

There is always more to learn about any topic. But we have created a skeleton and given it a shape, and now you are in a position to build on it. In Chapter 10, we will look at some of the best practices involved in using Apache log4j.

.

CHAPTER 10

■ ■ ■

Best Practices and Looking Forward to 1.3

In this book, I have discussed the most popular Java-based logging API to date: Apache log4j. Remember, logging is not the primary goal of most applications. It is there only to help us follow the internal status of the application. It helps us detect problems faster, publish messages to determine how the system is functioning, and maintain and debug the application with less time and cost. On the other hand, using logging incorrectly might affect the speed and function of an application. Hence, great care is needed in choosing the right components for the logging process and the best way to use those components. It is also very important to check that custom logging components do not affect the speed and integrity of existing components in any way.

The role of logging changes as an application progresses from development to production. At the development stage, logging information is targeted toward the developer checking, debugging, and finalizing the code. At the production stage, it is important to know what the application is doing as a whole. Such considerations affect the choice of priority for particular logging information. At the production stage, critical information such as warnings and errors are important, whereas debug information is more important at the development stage.

In this chapter, I will discuss a few points that are critical to the performance of logging, and compare log4j to the JDK logging API in terms of their internal workings and performance so that when it comes time to implement logging in your own applications, you know which API best serves your needs. Finally, I will present some of the features we can expect to see in the forthcoming 1.3 release of log4j. These new features will certainly provide more power to the developer community to meet complicated logging requirements.

Obtaining a Logger

In log4j, the entry point to the logging framework is the Logger object. We obtain an instance of the Logger object and ask it to log different messages with different levels. To work in log4j, loggers must have names. What naming convention should be used for these Logger objects?

There is no strict rule about what a logger's name should be. Still, we need to take great care in choosing a naming convention for the Logger objects in our applications. We configure a Logger through the configuration file. How do we know which application component is using which Logger object? How will it impact the whole application, if we change the configuration of a particular logger? Imagine that we have an application with hundreds of different components using a common logging configuration file. In this case, we would certainly need to come up with a naming strategy for Logger objects so that we know the individual loggers each component is using. By having a well-designed naming convention, it is easy for us to assess the impact of any change we make to a particular logger configuration.

■**Best Practice** Use a package-based naming convention for Logger objects.

One great idea for a naming convention is package-based naming. Generally, application components are divided into several packages. Each package contains related classes for certain aspects of the application. It is a good practice to use package name–based Logger objects, as this convention is easy to maintain.

■**Best Practice** For situations in which components in the same package require separate logging behavior, separate loggers on the basis of the tasks the components perform.

Immediately, the question arises of whether a package contains classes that perform several distinct activities. For example, the package com.apress.logging.log4j.util can contain many utility classes. If all of them are using the same logger named com.apress.logging.log4j.util, then changing the configuration for this logger will affect all the utilities within this package. This may be undesirable. For example, one of the classes in the util package may be writing data to a file, and another class may be sending data to a remote TCP/IP server. We might need detailed logging enabled for the class doing TCP/IP, but may not need the same level of detailed logging for the class doing file I/O. In such situations, it may be helpful to use two different loggers and name them according to the job they do.

The main point is to come up with an appropriate naming convention for loggers used within an application. This will increase the maintainability of the loggers. Also, it will help prevent a configuration change in one logger from affecting the others.

Using Logger Hierarchy

Log4j supports logger hierarchy. The loggers are organized in a parent-child relationship. For example, a logger named com.foo is the parent logger of the logger com.foo.bar. In the logger hierarchy, the child logger inherits the properties and the logger components from its immediate parent. In short, this means that all the logging events captured by the child logger will be processed by the child logger itself and also by its parent logger. This may also mean that logging messages will appear twice if both the child and parent logger use the same logging destinations, which may be undesirable. Of course, in log4j, we can turn off the use of the parent logger in the hierarchy. You can do so via

```
setAdditivity(false);
```

or via the configuration file, add this line:

```
log4j.logger.[logger name].additivity=false
```

Again, there are situations in which we might want this logger hierarchy enabled.

▓**Best Practice** For situations in which one application component tries to log the same information to different destinations by using separate components belonging to the same package, try to use the logger hierarchy.

Imagine an order-processing application in which component A receives an order. It processes the order and now needs to store the order-specific logging information to a file and also wants to send the same information back to a corporate logging database. Application component B writes the data to the local file and component C writes the logging information to the corporate database. The important point to consider is whether the application components A, B, and C belong to a package hierarchy. For example, components B and C may belong to package com.processor and component A may belong to package com.processor.order. Another component, D, might deal with e-mail–based orders and may be in package com.processor.order.email. In such situations, we are in a position to use the parent-child logger relationship.

We need to judge if the loggers are able to justify the parent-child relationship on the basis of logging activity, and not only by the package structure. If they are parent and child in terms of logging behavior, then use the relationship.

▓**Best Practice** If the logger hierarchy is turned on, the logging framework needs to determine the parent logger (recursively up the logger tree). This may reduce performance.

The benchmark result with log4j shows that walking through the logger hierarchy is three times slower than normal logging activity. So take great care in determining whether to use the logger hierarchy in your applications. The examples provided in this book aim to keep the parent-child relationship turned off unless it is necessary to demonstrate how the relationship works.

Logging Messages Efficiently

What to log and how to log? The answers to these questions determine how effective a particular application's logging is. Choose carefully and come up with a strategy as to what information is needed for debugging and what information is needed for routine maintenance. Decide carefully where to log information. Decide the formatting of the log messages so that the information can be processed and analyzed in the future by other applications.

▓**Best Practice** Avoid logging unnecessary information. This will convolute the logging trace and make it harder to analyze.

Redundant and unnecessary logging information affects an application's performance and usefulness. Even if we use a level that is turned off in the deployed application, the logger framework will have to do the extra work of checking the levels for each logging message. This level checking for logging requests with redundant and unnecessary information will affect the performance of the overall logging. So it is best to avoid having such logging requests within an application.

▓Best Practice Avoid using parameter construction within the logging request.

When developing your own applications, you might think that you have avoided making unnecessary logging requests; however, you still may have a logging request that looks like the following:

```
logger.info("This is "+var1+" logging from the method"+var2);
```

The cost involved here is the parameter construction. Use simple Java techniques such as StringBuffer for the concatenation of String objects and avoid using "+" for joining two String objects, for example. A badly coded application might have several of these sorts of statements.

▓Best Practice Check if logging is enabled before you try to log.

Suppose we have an application that logs all the entries of a list of customer orders (highly unlikely!). All information with a level of DEBUG is printed:

```
ArrayList list;
int length = list.size();

for(int k=0;k<size;k++)
{
    logger.debug("The customer: "+ ( (Customer)list.get(k) ).toString() );
}
```

What happens if the DEBUG level is turned off? Inside the for loop, the parameter construction will still take place, the logger will check if the DEBUG level is enabled, and if not, it will discard the request. To avoid this sort of situation, we could write

```
if(logger.isDebugEnabled())
{
    //do the for loop here
}
```

This will save the cost of unnecessary parameter construction. On the other hand, if the DEBUG level is turned on, there may be an extra cost for evaluating whether the DEBUG level is enabled. But this is insignificant overhead compared to the parameter construction, as it takes about 1 percent of the time of actual logging.

Issues with Localization

The localization of logging information through the `java.util.ResourceBundle` object is a great feature for publishing logging information in different languages. However, the decision to use the localization feature within log4j can be tricky.

■**Best Practice** Do not use `ResourceBundle` objects when you are not using the localization feature.

Constructing and using `ResourceBundle` objects is costly. If your application is presently supporting only one language, refrain from using localization within your code. You can always enable this feature in the future to support different languages.

Using Location Information

Log4j supports location information for a logging request. The log4j API tries to detect the exact line number of the code from which the logging request was issued.

■**Best Practice** Determining location information is costly. It is best to avoid this in application logging, if possible.

Dynamic location information generation is not reliable. It might not work properly with many compilers that use optimization techniques. Moreover, it takes a great deal of overhead for the logging framework to go through the stack trace to determine location information.

Formatting Logging Information

The formatting of logging information is important. On one hand, the more information, the better. On the other hand, each bit of information costs CPU memory. We need to carefully determine the formatting of logging information. XML formatting is costlier than simple text-based output, but the benefit of XML-formatted logging information is that it's more reusable and portable.

`PatternLayout` objects in log4j provide extreme flexibility in terms of defining the elements of the final logging information and the formatting instructions. Using `PatternLayout`, we can precisely control the content of the logging information in any destination. For XML/HTML-based logging information, we need to use separate `Layout` objects. `PatternLayout` is responsible for formatting the content of the logging information and is not involved in the presentation of that information.

Dates are one of the main concerns when it comes to formatting, as they are complicated and slow down the logging performance. The log4j API provides several date formatting objects such as `DateLayout` and `ISO8601DateFormat`. The `ISO8601DateFormat` is the cheapest and fastest of all the date formats available.

Using Renderer Objects

In log4j, `Renderer` objects are used to construct a `String` representation of any `Object` passed to the logging framework.

▓**Best Practice** `Renderer` objects follow a class hierarchy. Any superclass `Renderer` is capable of rendering the subclass.

For example, if we have a `VehicleRenderer` object, it will be able to render the `Car` object so long as `Car` is a subclass of `Vehicle`.

▓**Best Practice** For a specialized rendering with the subclass, register a subclass-specific `Renderer`. In such cases, the superclass `Renderer` is not invoked.

For example, we could register a `CarRenderer` object to render all the `Car` objects, in which case `VehicleRenderer` will not be used to render the `Car` objects.

Using Asynchronous Logging

The log4j API offers the `AsyncAppender` object to perform asynchronous logging. This object stores logging events in a bounded buffer and releases the events when the maximum buffer size is reached.

▓**Best Practice** `AsyncAppender` does not always increase performance.

If the bounded buffer gets filled up quickly, then there is extra overhead for managing the bounded buffer, which slows down performance. But `AsyncAppender` is quite effective in situations involving long blocking networks, I/O access, or less CPU-intensive operations.

Using Filter Objects

In the examples of `Filter` objects in our log4j discussion in Chapter 5, you saw that they are useful for filtering a logging request against some application-specific criteria other than the logging level. You also learned how filter chaining makes it possible to check a logging request against multiple criteria.

But filter chaining involves loading more than one `Filter` object and invoking the `decide()` method in each of them to filter the logging request. One alternative we demonstrated in Chapter 7 is to write a custom `Filter` object.

■**Best Practice** Try to do as much possible in one `Filter` object.

For situations in which you need to create multiple custom `Filter` objects, try to design them in such a way that one `Filter` object can serve various common filtering purposes. No doubt, embedding various application logics within one `Filter` object makes it difficult to reuse and restricts it to a particular application scenario. Still, this is worth considering in some situations.

Imagine we are trying to log information to a file. We want to perform checks against whether the logging event was generated from a certain application and also if it has the necessary security privileges to do the file I/O. In theory, we can come up with two `Filter` objects: one for checking the origin of the application and the other for checking the permissions. This way, we have two reusable `Filter` objects for event origin checking and file I/O permission checking, which is good. But if we are not writing generic logging components to be used by other applications, this might be unnecessary. Try to combine both checking processes within one `Filter` object. This will save the time it takes to load and invoke two `Filter` objects.

The design of `Filter` objects is specific to an application and often requires patience and time to decide how to design the `Filter` objects. Sometimes, you might need to come up with generic `Filter` objects reusable by many other application components, and sometimes you will write `Filter` objects specific to one application area. You need to make a trade-off before you decide to write single or multiple `Filter` objects.

Using Nested Diagnostic Context

The log4j API provides Nested Diagnostic Context (NDC) objects to populate the logging information with client-specific information. For example, server-based applications handling multiple clients (Java Servlet technology is an example) often require that logging traces produced by different client activities be differentiated.

■**Best Practice** To distinguish clients in server-side components handling multiple clients, use NDC.

The whole idea of NDC is to include unique client-specific information. Take care in deciding which information to put in the NDC, and its degree of uniqueness.

Configuration Issues

The log4j API supports both properties-style and XML-style configuration files. There is also a programmatic way of configuring every log4j component. But programmatic configuration is impossible to change without modifying the source code. To benefit from the highly configurable nature of log4j, we must configure log4j via a configuration file.

Not all the components in log4j are configurable through the properties style. So it is more often a good practice to use an XML-style configuration file.

If you ever need to change the configuration while your system is up and running, you must implement the `configureAndWatch` options for the log4j configuration. This way you can change the configuration file without bringing down the system. The log4j framework will look for any configuration change in a specified time interval (the default is 60 seconds) and reinitialize the framework if the configuration has changed.

The `configureAndWatch` property can be used by calling

```
PropertyConfigurator.configureAndWatch(props);
```

or

```
DOMConfigurator.configureAndWatch(configFileName);
```

at the starting point of an application. The log4j framework will use the same configuration file to configure itself, only with an extra feature that watches for any configuration change. This often proves quite useful when using log4j in server-based applications for situations in which it may be difficult to bring down the server for every logging configuration change.

Comparing log4j and the JDK Logging API

Perhaps you have noticed the startling similarities between the log4j and JDK logging implementations. They share the same basic components, such as `Logger`, `Level`, `Appender/Handler`, and `Layout/Formatter`. The two APIs also strongly resemble each other in their internal architecture. However, a few basic differences are worth mentioning, and some of them may be critical when choosing one logging API over the other. Table 10-1 summarizes the difference between these two logging APIs, and each point is discussed in more detail subsequently.

Table 10-1. *Comparison Between the JDK Logging API and Apache log4j*

Features	JDK Logging API	Apache log4j
Configuration	The JDK logging API starts with a default configuration file supplied by JDK. In the JDK logging API, the configuration order in a configuration file is sequential. The parent logger must be configured before the child logger. The JDK logging API supports only properties-style configuration.	Apache log4j does not assume any default configuration. It looks for a `log4j.properties` or `log4j.xml` file in the classpath to initialize itself. In log4j, the order of configuration has no impact on the initialization. Apache log4j supports both properties- and XML-style configuration.
Formatting of logging information	The JDK logging API renders logging information only in text format or XML format.	Apache log4j supports a wide variety of output formats such as HTML, XML, text, etc. The content of the logging information can be controlled by specifying patterns.
Output destination	The JDK logging API supports only sockets, consoles, files, and memory buffers as output destinations.	Apache log4j supports a much wider variety of logging destinations, including JMSs and databases, as well as protocols such as Telnet, SMTP, etc.

Features	JDK Logging API	Apache log4j
Filtering	The JDK logging API allows attaching filters to Logger and Handler objects. Filter chaining to filter against multiple criteria is not possible with the JDK logging API.	Apache log4j attaches filters to Appender objects only. Apache log4j supports filter chaining.
Location information	The JDK logging API automatically tries to determine the location information for the logging request. There is no way to control this behavior.	In log4j, location information can be configured to be included in the logging information or not.
Error handling	The JDK logging API throws back any runtime exceptions to the caller application. This may cause the application to crash unless these exceptions are handled.	In log4j, errors are handled internally without throwing them back to the caller application. This makes the application and the logging function independent of each other.

Comparing Configuration Options

Unlike log4j, JDK ships with a default logging configuration file for the logging API. Even application developers need not define any custom configuration file; the JDK logging API will configure itself with the default configuration file. However, log4j does not make any assumption about the logging environment. If a configuration file is not found in the classpath of the execution environment, log4j fails to initialize properly.

In terms of configuration options, log4j is much more versatile in that it supports both properties-style and XML-style configuration. The JDK logging API supports only properties-style configuration.

Also, the JDK logging configuration is sequential—that is, the order of configuration matters. For example, look at the following configuration order:

```
a.b.level=SEVERE
a.level=INFO
```

You might be surprised to discover that the logger a.b will be assigned its parent logger's level INFO. This is because the parent logger has been configured after the child logger, and the configurations for all the child loggers have been updated according to the configuration of the parent logger. Thus, in the JDK logging API, the settings for the child loggers should appear after the settings of the parent logger. The parent logger updates the settings of its child loggers.

The log4j configuration is independent of the order. In log4j, the child loggers automatically inherit from their immediate parent logger by traversing the hierarchy upward.

Formatting Logging Information: Comparing Formatter and Layout Objects

Both logging APIs provide mechanisms to format the logging information to be produced. In log4j, these objects are called Layout objects, and in the JDK logging API, they are called Formatter objects. The JDK logging API, however, provides only two Formatter objects: SimpleFormatter and XMLFormatter. The log4j API provides a vast range of Layout objects capable of formatting information in various formats, such as HTML, XML, and text. The log4j API also provides PatternLayout, which is a powerful mechanism for including or excluding various parts of logging events in the final logging output.

Output Destination: Comparing Handler and Appender Objects

The JDK logging API provides `Handler` objects to publish logging information to a preferred destination. Similarly, log4j provides `Appender` objects to publish logging information. Currently, the JDK logging API can publish only to consoles, files, sockets, and memory buffers. However, log4j provides more choices for logging destinations. With log4j, we can publish logging information to various destinations, such as consoles, files, databases, JMSs, NT event logs, UNIX Syslogs, and so on.

Of course, both APIs can be extended to provide any number of customized `Handler` and `Formatter` objects to support logging to any other application-specific destination. But by default, log4j covers almost all commonly required logging destinations.

Comparing Filter Objects

The JDK logging API offers the facility to attach `Filter` objects to `Logger` and `Handler` objects. With the help of `Filter` objects, it is possible to obtain more fine-grained control over logging decisions. The JDK logging API allows only one `Filter` object to be associated with a logger.

With log4j, `Filter` objects can be attached only to `Appender` objects. But log4j offers more capabilities with its `Filter` objects. As I discussed in Chapter 5, it is possible to chain several `Filter` objects to accomplish complex logging tasks. We can also configure more than one `Filter` object for a particular `Appender` object. The JDK logging API lacks these `Filter` object features. A `Filter` object in the JDK logging API can either accept or reject a logging request, but it cannot ignore a logging request and delegate it to any other `Filter` objects. Thus, `Filter` chaining is not possible with the JDK logging API.

Comparing Location Information Options

The JDK logging API and log4j both are capable of producing information about the location from which the logging request was generated. However, the production of location information is very costly in terms of performance.

In log4j, we can enable or disable location information according to the application's needs. By default, location information is not part of the logging output. We can enable it by specifying the location information attribute in the `PatternLayout` object as described in Chapter 4.

Unlike log4j, the JDK logging API always tries to determine the location information, and this cannot be avoided. Also, the techniques that the JDK logging API uses for dynamic location information generation are not totally reliable. Normally, this is done by analyzing the stack trace of the application. But many compilers employ different optimization techniques that may cause this stack trace analysis to fail or produce incorrect information. Thus, application developers tend to avoid including location information as a part of the logging output.

Comparing Error Handling

The main drawback of the JDK logging API is that it throws `RunTimeExceptions` back to the caller classes in the application. If these exceptions are not handled within the application, the application will crash. It's particularly undesirable if the application is crashing because of a problem with the logging rather than a problem with the application itself.

The log4j API is more elegant in handling the errors and exceptions generated in the logging operation. All `Appender` objects in log4j have an associated `ErrorHandler` object. `ErrorHandler` objects such as `OnlyOnceErrorHandler` produce a message to the console on the first occurrence of an error and ignore the following errors. This enables the application to continue functioning normally even when there is a problem with the logging. The problem with the logging function can be detected by analyzing the console messages and then corrected eventually.

Log4j also makes it possible to define customized error-handling components that can perform all sorts of operations to handle the error condition gracefully. The change of error-handling strategy can be achieved simply by changing the configuration file to use any ErrorHandler object, and requires no coding change at all.

Looking Forward to log4j 1.3

Log4j version 1.3 will be released in the near future. This release promises to incorporate many new features, improvements to the performance, and better configurability and extendibility. I will introduce the new features of log4j 1.3 in the following sections.

> **■Note** Existing applications using log4j will still work well with the new 1.3 release, as long as those applications do not use any previously deprecated objects.

Joran Configurator

A new XML-based configurator will be introduced with the log4j 1.3 release. It will eventually replace the DOMConfigurator. The Joran Configurator can be taught new configuration rules at runtime, without recompilation. The concept of the Joran Configurator is based on the commons-digester. The main difference is that Joran treats the XML configuration as a DOM tree rather than Simple API for XML (SAX) events, and supports implicit actions. Implicit actions are executed when no explicit rule applies.

Plug-ins

Plug-ins will be introduced in the 1.3 release of log4j. Plug-ins extend the standard features provided by log4j, and will be configurable via the XML files. Each plug-in operates against a particular LoggingRepository. These plug-ins can be started, stopped, and managed programmatically. The two types of plug-ins available within log4j version 1.3 are receivers and watchdogs.

Receivers

Receivers are the opposite of Appender objects; they receive the logging events as opposed to publishing them. The most important role of receivers is to listen to external events and bring them into log4j to deal with them. For example, SocketReceiver or JMSReceiver can listen to remote logging events and bring them into the log4j environment to deal with them.

Watchdogs

Watchdogs are plug-ins that extend the concepts of monitoring the configuration source change. In traditional log4j (up to version 1.2.x), the configureAndWatch() method is used to start a thread to monitor any change in the configuration source file. The watchdogs will have the following advantages over the traditional configureAndWatch() method:

- Watchdogs can be started and stopped programmatically.

- Watchdogs can be configured via the log4j configuration file.

- Watchdogs can deal with different sources of configuration data. For instance, `HttpWatchDog` can deal with modified data over an HTTP connection, whereas `FileWatchDog` can deal with file changes.

More Filters

Log4j version 1.3 introduces many useful filters, including the following:

- `MDCMatchFilter`: Filter based on the key-value pairs in an MDC at the time of the logging event.

- `NDCMatchFilter`: Filter based on the NDC at the time of the logging event.

- `MessageMatchFilter`: Filter based on the content of the log messages.

Conclusion

I hope the topics we've covered provide you with a solid foundation for working with the most popular logging API—Apache log4j. The final two parts of the book, Appendixes A and B, provide a brief comparison of log4j against the standard JDK logging API. Both are well-designed and easy to use. Considering the present status of both APIs, log4j, in my opinion, has a slight edge. But you are not always going to need such a sophisticated logging mechanism. The important point is to understand that every day, software applications are becoming more and more business-critical. In this context, an application with better maintainability and quick-fix capability wins. A well-planned logging framework within an application will no doubt help it gain some advantage in a competitive market. Hence, it is time for all of us to reconsider the importance of logging in our applications.

This chapter introduced the features that will be added to the 1.3 release of log4j. As this book is being written, version 1.3 is in its alpha stage. We hope it will be released soon. Its new features and improvements will surely make it very popular in the developer community.

As feedback flows to Sun and Apache for their logging APIs, we will see even more improvements and features being incorporated within log4j. Whatever these new features may be, the basics presented in this book will remain the same, and I hope this book will prove useful to you now and in the future.

APPENDIX A

■■■

The log4j Configuration Parameters

Table A-1 presents all the configurable components in log4j and the configurable parameters associated with each component.

Table A-1. *Log4j Framework Configuration*

Component	Configuration Parameters
log4j	Renderer Appender Logger Root LoggerFactory (CategoryFactory)
Renderer	RenderedClass RenderingClass
Appender	ErrorHandler Param Layout Filter Appender-ref Name Class
Layout	Param Class
Filter	Param Class
ErrorHandler	Param Root-ref Logger-ref Appender-ref Class
Level	Param Class Value
Logger	Name Class Additivity (true|false); default true

Table A-2 presents all the Appender objects and their configurable parameters.

Table A-2. *Log4j Appenders and Their Configuration Parameters*

Appender	Configuration Parameters
ConsoleAppender	ImmediateFlush Encoding Threshold Target Name Layout ErrorHandler
FileAppender	ImmediateFlush Encoding Threshold Filename FileAppend BufferedIO BufferSize Name Layout ErrorHandler
RollingFileAppender	All properties of FileAppender MaxFileSize MaxBackupIndex
JDBCAppender	BufferSize Driver Layout User Password URL SQL Name ErrorHandler
JMSAppender	InitialContextFactoryName LocationInfo Username Password ProviderURL SecurityCredentials SecurityPrincipalName TopicBindingName TopicConnectionFactoryBindingName URLPkgPrefixes Name Layout ErrorHandler
SocketAppender	LocationInfo Port ReconnectionDelay RemoteHost Name ErrorHandler Layout

Appender	Configuration Parameters
NTEventLogAppender	Source Name Layout ErrorHandler
SMTPAppender	BufferSize EvaluatorClass From To LocationInfo SMTPHost Subject Name Layout ErrorHandler
TelnetAppender	Port Name Layout ErrorHandler

Table A-3 presents all the Layout objects and their configurable parameters.

Table A-3. *Log4j Layouts and Their Configuration Parameters*

Layout	Configuration Parameters
TTCCLayout	CategoryPrefixing ContextPrinting ThreadPrinting
HTMLLayout	LocationInfo Title
PatternLayout	ConversionPattern

The log4j DTD

Listing B-1 presents the complete Document Type Definition (DTD) for the log4j configuration.

Listing B-1. *The log4j DTD*

```
<?xml version="1.0" encoding="UTF-8" ?>

<!-- Version: 1.2 -->

<!-- A configuration element consists of optional renderer
elements,appender elements, categories and an optional root
element. -->

<!ELEMENT log4j:configuration (renderer*, appender*,(category|logger)*,root?,
                              categoryFactory?)>


<!ATTLIST log4j:configuration
  xmlns:log4j           CDATA #FIXED "http://jakarta.apache.org/log4j/"
  threshold             (all|debug|info|warn|error|fatal|off|null) "null"
  debug                 (true|false|null)  "null">

<!-- renderer elements allow the user to customize the conversion of  -->
<!-- message objects to String. -->

<!ELEMENT renderer EMPTY>
<!ATTLIST renderer
  renderedClass   CDATA #REQUIRED
  renderingClass CDATA #REQUIRED>

<!-- Appenders must have a name and a class. -->
<!-- Appenders may contain an error handler, a layout, optional parameters -->
<!-- and filters. They may also reference (or include) other appenders. -->
```

```
<!ELEMENT appender (errorHandler?, param*, layout?, filter*, appender-ref*)>
<!ATTLIST appender
  name    ID #REQUIRED
  class   CDATA #REQUIRED>

<!ELEMENT layout (param*)>
<!ATTLIST layout
  class   CDATA #REQUIRED>

<!ELEMENT filter (param*)>
<!ATTLIST filter
  class   CDATA #REQUIRED>

<!-- ErrorHandlers can be of any class. They can admit any number of -->
<!-- parameters. -->

<!ELEMENT errorHandler (param*, root-ref?, logger-ref*,  appender-ref?)>
<!ATTLIST errorHandler
    class         CDATA #REQUIRED >

<!ELEMENT root-ref EMPTY>

<!ELEMENT logger-ref EMPTY>
<!ATTLIST logger-ref
  ref IDREF #REQUIRED>

<!ELEMENT param EMPTY>
<!ATTLIST param
  name  CDATA #REQUIRED
  value CDATA #REQUIRED>


<!-- The priority class is org.apache.log4j.Level by default -->
<!ELEMENT priority (param*)>
<!ATTLIST priority
  class   CDATA #IMPLIED
  value   CDATA #REQUIRED>

<!-- The level class is org.apache.log4j.Level by default -->
<!ELEMENT level (param*)>
<!ATTLIST level
  class   CDATA #IMPLIED
  value   CDATA #REQUIRED>
```

```
<!-- If no level element is specified, then the configurator MUST not -->
<!-- touch the level of the named category. -->
<!ELEMENT category (param*,(priority|level)?,appender-ref*)>
<!ATTLIST category
  class       CDATA #IMPLIED
  name        CDATA #REQUIRED
  additivity (true|false) "true"  >


<!-- If no level element is specified, then the configurator MUST not -->
<!-- touch the level of the named logger. -->
<!ELEMENT logger (level?,appender-ref*)>
<!ATTLIST logger
  name   ID #REQUIRED
  additivity (true|false) "true"  >



<!ELEMENT categoryFactory (param*)>
<!ATTLIST categoryFactory
    class        CDATA #REQUIRED>


<!ELEMENT appender-ref EMPTY>
<!ATTLIST appender-ref
  ref IDREF #REQUIRED>


<!-- If no priority element is specified, then the configurator MUST not -->
<!-- touch the priority of root. -->
<!-- The root category always exists and cannot be subclassed. -->
<!ELEMENT root (param*, (priority|level)?, appender-ref*)>



<!-- ================================================================= -->
<!--                     A logging event                             -->
<!-- ================================================================= -->
<!ELEMENT log4j:eventSet (log4j:event*)>
<!ATTLIST log4j:eventSet
  xmlns:log4j           CDATA #FIXED "http://jakarta.apache.org/log4j/"
  version               (1.1|1.2) "1.2"
  includesLocationInfo  (true|false) "true">



<!ELEMENT log4j:event (log4j:message, log4j:NDC?, log4j:throwable?,
                       log4j:locationInfo?) >
```

```
<!-- The timestamp format is application dependent. -->
<!ATTLIST log4j:event
    logger     CDATA #REQUIRED
    level      CDATA #REQUIRED
    thread     CDATA #REQUIRED
    timestamp  CDATA #REQUIRED>

<!ELEMENT log4j:message (#PCDATA)>
<!ELEMENT log4j:NDC (#PCDATA)>

<!ELEMENT log4j:throwable (#PCDATA)>

<!ELEMENT log4j:locationInfo EMPTY>
<!ATTLIST log4j:locationInfo
  class  CDATA #REQUIRED
  method CDATA #REQUIRED
  file   CDATA #REQUIRED
  line   CDATA #REQUIRED >
```

Index

forums.apress.com

JOIN THE APRESS FORUMS AND BE PART OF OUR COMMUNITY. You'll find discussions that cover topics of interest to IT professionals, programmers, and enthusiasts just like you. If you post a query to one of our forums, you can expect that some of the best minds in the business—especially Apress authors, who all write with *The Expert's Voice*™—will chime in to help you. Why not aim to become one of our most valuable participants (MVPs) and win cool stuff? Here's a sampling of what you'll find:

DATABASES

Data drives everything.

Share information, exchange ideas, and discuss any database programming or administration issues.

INTERNET TECHNOLOGIES AND NETWORKING

Try living without plumbing (and eventually IPv6).

Talk about networking topics including protocols, design, administration, wireless, wired, storage, backup, certifications, trends, and new technologies.

JAVA

We've come a long way from the old Oak tree.

Hang out and discuss Java in whatever flavor you choose: J2SE, J2EE, J2ME, Jakarta, and so on.

MAC OS X

All about the Zen of OS X.

OS X is both the present and the future for Mac apps. Make suggestions, offer up ideas, or boast about your new hardware.

OPEN SOURCE

Source code is good; understanding (open) source is better.

Discuss open source technologies and related topics such as PHP, MySQL, Linux, Perl, Apache, Python, and more.

PROGRAMMING/BUSINESS

Unfortunately, it is.

Talk about the Apress line of books that cover software methodology, best practices, and how programmers interact with the "suits."

WEB DEVELOPMENT/DESIGN

Ugly doesn't cut it anymore, and CGI is absurd.

Help is in sight for your site. Find design solutions for your projects and get ideas for building an interactive Web site.

SECURITY

Lots of bad guys out there—the good guys need help.

Discuss computer and network security issues here. Just don't let anyone else know the answers!

TECHNOLOGY IN ACTION

Cool things. Fun things.

It's after hours. It's time to play. Whether you're into LEGO® MINDSTORMS™ or turning an old PC into a DVR, this is where technology turns into fun.

WINDOWS

No defenestration here.

Ask questions about all aspects of Windows programming, get help on Microsoft technologies covered in Apress books, or provide feedback on any Apress Windows book.

HOW TO PARTICIPATE:

Go to the Apress Forums site at **http://forums.apress.com/**.

Click the New User link.

CPSIA information can be obtained at www.ICGtesting.com
Printed in the USA
LVOW112348310712

292438LV00013B/52/A